Brunel University Library

Youth in New Society

YOUTH IN NEW SOCIETY

Edited and with an introduction by

TIMOTHY RAISON

RUPERT HART-DAVIS
Soho Square · London · W1
1966

Made and printed in Great Britain
by The Garden City Press Limited,
Letchworth, Hertfordshire

Contents

Introduction

To mirror, to analyse, to understand, not to exhort or moralize—this
has been the aim of *New Society* since it was launched in October, 1962.
At times it has disappointed people who have felt that, with our title,
we should prescribe the formula for a better world. Often, too, we
have let down those who want to know the answer to a particular
social problem. But that is the fault of the social and human sciences as
much as ours. Inevitably at this stage of their development the conclusion of any particular study is liable to be, "We don't know. We
need more research".

Yet, for all the uncertainties and the patchy nature of the data, some
sort of picture of our times does seem to emerge: for all their im-
maturity the social sciences look full of promise. And some at least of
that promise seems to us to have spilled over into the pages of
New Society. Certainly, an encouraging feature of the journal's progress
has been the discovery that there is much more of interest going on in
the admittedly wide field which we cover than we—and many of our
well-wishers—ever expected.

Not that we confine ourselves to academic researches. We have
always held that there is a place in *New Society* for detailed rapportage
and descriptive writing that will complement the findings of the
researchers. One sign that we have been justified in this belief is the
fact that our journalistic pieces as well as our scholarly pieces have

often provided source material for other publications and for broadcasting.

Of no subject we cover has all this been more true than that of youth. The youth question—and whether there is a youth question—has dominated much discussion about society in the past year or two. Juvenile delinquency, juvenile sexual behaviour, juvenile ethics, juvenile culture, juvenile spending, the gulf between the generations—these are the themes that have recurred over and over again in writing, broadcasting, conferences and private conversation. Even if we had wanted to, we could not have prevented them occurring again and again in the pages of *New Society*.

Society's uncertainties about the springs of behaviour in the young are at least as great as they are about any other contemporary trend. Yet on looking back at what we have published in our first two and a half years, it seemed to me that there was among it enough illuminating material on youth and its characteristics and problems to provide a worthwhile first *New Society* anthology.

It follows the blend of research and descriptive writing that I have just described. It is typical in that it contains a medley of varying views rather than a *New Society* line. It is also typical in the way in which the articles came to be published. Sometimes the theme was thought up by us and presented to an academic. Sometimes we heard of a piece of research which had just been completed and spurred or cajoled its author into writing it up for us. In one case, the study of the Margate offenders, the research was set up and carried out by us, with the aid of generous backing from Mr Sidney Bernstein and Granada Television.

Sometimes pieces came out of the blue. Alec MacGuire's perceptive study of Mods and Rockers was one instance: its ideas have since passed into wide currency. Pippa Phemister's moving story of an experiment with puppets among teenagers was another. Two more spectacular examples were Neale Pharoah's account of his experiences in a detention centre, which led to his inclusion on Mr Henry Brooke's admittedly short-lived advisory council on juvenile delinquency, and the account of how Beat killed the gangs on Merseyside—an article which was seized on by television and much of the national press.

These two articles illustrate another of our aims—not only to get social scientists and reporters to write about "people", but also to get "people" to write about themselves. And this is true of another contributor, Ray Gosling, who is, of course, a professional writer; but his special ability is to echo his generation—its incoherence as well as its volubility. He does so, I think, with a touch of poetry in "The Tough and the Tender"; and it is the interplay of such pieces with the more formal academic investigations and speculations that will give this book such value as it has.

Timothy Raison, 1965

The material on which the three articles by E.M. and M. Eppel are based is to be published in revised and expanded form in "Age of Uncertainty" (Routledge and Kegan Paul).

1

Adolescence: 12 to 18
The body
W A MARSHALL

19 NOVEMBER 1964

NUMBER OF DEATHS IN BRITAIN FROM VARIOUS CAUSES IN THE 10–20 AGE GROUP 1961; AND COMPARISON OF INCIDENCE WITH SIX OTHER AGE GROUPS*

all causes	5,054	5*
bacteria and viruses	90	6
neoplasms	116	7
endocrine, nutritional, blood	110	6
respiration, circulation, digestion, genitourinary system	551	6
skin and bones	53	3
congenital malformations	193	4
accidents, poisonings, violence	1,586	5
mental, nervous system	230	6

The period of life between the 12th and 18th years might be described as the period of male ascendancy. At birth, boys tend to be slightly bigger in most dimensions than girls but the difference is only of the order of 1 to 3 per cent in stature and the length of limbs. The earlier adolescence of girls makes them bigger and stronger than boys between

* E.g. "5" here means that of the seven age groups this one ranks fifth in the number of deaths from this cause.

I

the ages of about 10½ and 13, but when the boys have their adolescent spurt, they grow far more than the girls did and finish up some 10 per cent bigger.

The relative effect of the adolescent spurt on different parts of the body varies between the two sexes and it is this variation which leads to many of the characteristic differences in body shape between men and women. The width of the hips increases as much in girls as in boys, but in all other dimensions there is a far greater increase in the male. The breadth of the shoulders and the breadth of the chest have particularly big increases in boys. The amount of bone and muscle in a boy's body increases greatly at adolescence but fat is lost. In girls there is little increase in bone diameter and fat is put on.

While the changes in size and shape which are characteristic of adolescence are taking place, there are also less obvious but equally important changes within the body. These physiological changes take place at the same time as the external ones so that they occur early in those who have an early adolescence and late in those who have a late adolescence. Their overall effect is greatly to increase the strength of the individual and his capacity for physical exertion.

For example the rise in blood pressure which has been going on steadily throughout childhood accelerates sharply at adolescence so that final adult values are quickly reached. This rise is greater in boys than in girls so that adult men have a slightly higher blood pressure than women. The heart rate becomes gradually slower throughout growth. In boys the number of red cells in the blood rises markedly at the time of adolescence and the amount of haemoglobin, the substance which carries oxygen, is also increased. The total volume of blood in the body also increases to a greater extent in boys than in girls.

In addition, the normal rate of breathing decreases throughout childhood and on through puberty in both sexes; but the maximum amount of air which can be breathed in a given time, or at a single breath, increases markedly in adolescent boys while there is little, if any, increase in girls. Moreover, the amount of air which must be taken into the lungs in order to pass a given amount of oxygen to the blood becomes less in boys than in girls. There is a further mechanism whereby, during severe exercise, the muscles can function even with an inadequate supply of oxygen by producing lactic acid and incurring what is known as an "oxygen debt". This mechanism improves in efficiency at adolescence and continues to improve at least until the age of 19 years. As a result of all these changes more oxygen can be made available to exercising muscle while the muscles themselves become capable of greater activity even beyond the limits of their increased oxygen supply. The total capacity for physical work is thus increased enormously in boys and to a lesser extent in girls.

The strength of the muscles increases to an even greater extent than their increasing size would suggest. Both the strength of arm thrust and the strength of arm pull become much greater in boys as their shoulder, back and chest muscles grow. These changes are less marked in girls. The strength of hand grip is greater in boys even before puberty because boys' forearms are bigger from the time of birth onwards. Both boys and girls show a marked increase at adolescence in the distance which they can put a 12 lb shot and boys also show a marked improvement in their running ability. There is good evidence that greater gains in strength occur in the spring than in the winter. A similar seasonal effect on growth in height can be seen at all ages.

It is said that menarche marks approximately the end of the increase of strength in girls and it is true that girls' performances in many athletic events seem to deteriorate after the age of 14 or 15. This may simply be because girls have less motivation to do well at this type of task as they grow up.

STRENGTH AND HEIGHT

An important aspect of the adolescent spurt in strength is that it may not occur for some time after the spurt in height. Growth in the size of the muscles is, however, only delayed by a very short time in relation to the height spurt so that the muscles grow first in size and only later in strength and there may be a gap of a year or more between the time when a boy reaches almost adult stature and has the muscular appearance of a man, and the time when he has in fact attained something approaching adult strength. This has given rise to the popular notion of a boy outgrowing his strength. There is in fact no time during adolescence when strength is not increasing and it is certainly not true that the changes accompanying adolescence have any weakening effect.

The greatest improvement in boys' muscular co-ordination occurs at the same time as strength increases most rapidly and some time after the greatest growth in size has already taken place. This time lag has given rise to another popular misconception, that adolescents become less skilled, particularly in balance, while they are growing rapidly. There is no evidence to support this view and a more reasonable explanation of the adolescent's apparent clumsiness is that for a short period of time his skill is not as close to its maximum as his size, although it never becomes less.

The time which a boy takes to react to a sudden stimulus decreases markedly between the ages of 14 and 18. This change is of obvious value in sports and in types of work where quick reactions are necessary.

One of the most important aspects of male adolescence is the variability in the age at which it may occur. As with girls, there is a trend towards earlier maturation. Some 14 year old boys have reached sexual maturity and are virtually adult in size, strength, skill and outlook, while others of the same age are for practical purposes, small boys. There is a tendency for educational and other administrators to legislate for all boys of the same age as if they were physical and social equals while, in fact, a post-adolescent boy of 13 will be more at home with a group of older post-adolescent boys than will a 15 year old who is just entering puberty. The boy whose adolescence is late frequently suffers serious emotional disturbance because his associates of the same age are not only sexually mature but are far bigger and stronger than he is. When this boy eventually has his adolescent spurt he may well become a bigger and more manly individual than any of those whom he may in earlier years have envied.

By the age of 18 most girls have completed their growth and passed the stage at which their physical skills are greatest. Boys on the other hand are improving in all their physical attributes up to this age and further improvements are yet to come, although in size, strength and skill they have already surpassed all but the most exceptional girls.

Personality
DEREK MILLER
19 NOVEMBER 1964

Despite the chronological vagueness of the adolescent age period, it is nevertheless a specific period in human development in all cultures. It is characterized by increased conflict with oneself and the outside world; and a high growth potential, physically, intellectually and emotionally. The dilemma as to what is meant by adolescence has to an extent been resolved by young people who have created their own social norms and see themselves as adolescent while they are in their teens.

The first obvious attempt to differentiate between self and non-self, "me" and "them", occurs when a child at the age of 2 begins to defy parental authority and say "No". During adolescence the individual further differentiates himself from others. Relationships outside the family become intense, and, as part of the process of becoming individuals, the adolescent group, in particular boys, tends to separate out "we" and "they". Whether "they" are perceived as hostile depends partly on the attitudes of the outside world, partly on the adolescent's psychological maturity.

Early adolescence, 11 to 15 in girls, 12 to 16 in boys, corresponds with puberty. Because of the rapid acceleration of growth, especially of arms and legs and the size and shape of hands, feet and face, individuals feel their bodies as disharmonious and are no longer at ease with themselves. They are likely to become negativistic, questioning and defiant.

This behaviour is a necessary testing of the limits of control and freedom but it also represents a demand for both. This is the age of secrecy from adults, particularly parents, a part of a technique of emotional separation which allows for increasing independence. To adults the early adolescent may at times appear to be egoistic, vain, proud and aggressive; at others helpless and dependent. On the one hand he seems capable of loyalty, self-sacrifice and devotion; on the other of utter selfishness. It is also an age of movement, and physical activity is used both as a tension-relieving device and as a way of communicating with others.

For both sexes in early adolescence formal and informal group formation is common. Transient gang formation occurs particularly with boys, although its extent varies between social classes and from culture to culture. The individual boy is often quite exhibitionistic with his peers and talks freely with them of highly intimate problems.

Girls, on the other hand, become increasingly modest, and yet increasingly aware of the opposite sex. Groupings of girls are more apparent than real; unless they are forced to live in an artificial unisexual environment, their relationships with each other are only transient, if often intense.

In late adolescence, 15 to 19 in girls, 16 to 20 in boys, with its increasing harmony of bodily features, healthy adolescents are able increasingly to accept and come to terms with themselves and the demands of reality, and in turn they can appropriately modify the demands they make on society. Individual talents and interests flower. This is the Indian summer of youth and after its passing one has to begin to face the awareness of mortality.

In both early and late adolescence intense self-contradiction is often experienced. The adolescent loves and hates, communicates freely and yet, when feeling misunderstood, as abruptly withdraws. The individual is at once submissive and rebellious, ascetic and self-indulgent, selfish and idealistic. Full of energy at one moment, and the next feeling overwhelmingly lazy, the adolescent varies between optimism and a preoccupation with the drab desert of the world. He is often too absorbed with the discrepancy between how he feels himself to be and how others see him. Various roles in both fantasy and reality are tried on, rather as fashionable attire changes. Much of this alternation can be seen as an attempt to establish a secure identity.

The way a child is treated by parents and its identification with their perceived qualities assist the process by which the infant becomes a "masculine boy" or a "feminine girl". Both these factors apply again with renewed intensity in the development of the sexual identification of the adolescent. Because of the inner turmoil of the period, throughout adolescence it is necessary to test the strength of, and consolidate, this identification. By the time late adolescence supervenes the boy should be capable of mature physical relationships.

The first testing of oneself as a sexual male normally occurs, in our society, by the necessary process of masturbation with heterosexual fantasies. At first boys establish their feelings of masculinity in relationship to members of the same sex. This is done by comparing physical, sexual and intellectual prowess with one's age mates. Asexual love of one's own sex, which tends to be a male prerogative, may in relatively closed masculine societies become overtly sexual with episodes of mutual sexual exploration which do not necessarily lead to an ultimate homosexual inclination.

In our society, a boy's first relationship with a girl is likely to be transient and highly experimental. It is as if the girl is a medal which a boy wears to prove his masculinity to his peers. Although a boy usually realizes how hurtful this attitude is towards a girl, he is often all too willing to derogate her by discussing her real and fantasied promiscuity. This need to derogate women would appear to allow a boy to revenge himself unconsciously on a girl for her feminine productivity, with which he cannot compete.

In later adolescence the girl friend may still be used by a boy to show his male friends his potency, but this should be becoming a tender, private, meaningful relationship. Young men do not normally appear to be highly promiscuous; when sexual relationships occur they are felt to be intense and last for a considerable time, although they may be quite exhibitionistic.

The menarche provides for girls a dramatic proof of their femininity, and they appear to establish this from the outset largely in relationship to boys; although they may compare themselves physically with each other, particularly as regards breast development. Masturbation in girls would not appear to be as necessary for normal development as in boys.

Apart from other factors, such as envy of masculine status, a girl, who tries out her budding femininity in a one to one relationship with a boy, is far more likely to be emotionally hurt than he, because she is likely to "fall in love" and fantasy permanence to the relationship. Partially because of the different rates of psychological maturation of the sexes, partially because of social pressures, the boy is less likely to want this permanence and most unlikely to want marriage. Thus all too often the girl's attempt to use her femininity in a constructive way, in an interpersonal relationship, is thwarted and she is left, not only feeling unloved but also unlovely.

It is probably better in our society for the girl in early adolescence, frustrated in her attempts to establish close relationship with boys by her parents' refusal to give her the necessary freedom, to be angry with them; than for her to be given too much freedom and then be hurt.

In general terms adolescence begins with the onset of the wish to be emotionally independent and sexually active; it ends with the completion of sexual identification, a choice of profession and a place for oneself in society.

The adolescent must be looked at as an individual, but he or she is also a member of a family and of society at large.

IN THE FAMILY

The adolescent boy feels increasingly ready to abandon childhood security. He wishes for independence long before he is able to handle the complexities of modern living. These, plus his inner uncertainty, may from time to time force a boy to wish to abandon his desire for independent judgment and action. On such occasions, to maintain his integrity, he angrily tends to feel that his motives are misunderstood and unreasonable demands are being made upon him. On the other hand, all too often his demands are perceived as intolerably unrealistic by parents or society. One way in which parents deal with their anxiety and anger about this is to withdraw emotionally; they thus become unable to perceive in a constructive manner how much responsibility the adolescent is able to handle. This relative rejection is more likely because the adolescent often represents to the parents an unconscious sexual or aggressive threat.

In girls the balance between dependence and independence is weighed more heavily toward the former. They tend to confide more in their mothers than boys with either parent. They establish a separate identity from their mothers by being alternately, highly aggressive towards them, and then, by literally and metaphorically borrowing their mother's clothing.

Girls have a need to be looked after. Since society makes fewer economic demands on a girl, it is possible for her to stay at home and help with the house. If psychological illness comes as a psycho-social withdrawal, it is more socially acceptable than for boys. Thus if a girl does present herself to a doctor with a psychological illness, or to the courts as delinquent, she is probably more disturbed than the equivalent boy.

Parents, too, have their difficulties. The growing independent needs of an adolescent son or daughter represent to a mother a threat of potential unemployment from her vocation of mothering. Feeling devalued by herself, her family and society, mothers then often act to keep the adolescent dependent. In addition, fathers in their social prime as their children become adolescent have the particular problem of envying their sons' greater sexual freedom than they possessed. They are also uncomfortably aware of the sexuality of their daughters. It is not unusual for the onset of late adolescence in a child, with the individual's drive for freedom, to unveil a marital conflict that has been hidden by the joint parental task of husband and wife which has now been relatively lost.

Society may be permissive towards adolescence: the provocative behaviour of youth is sometimes tolerated. However, extreme inconsistences pervade society's attitude. Although standards are in a constant state of flux, society at large expects the adolescent to complete sexual identification without sexual experience, to make a choice of profession often with minimal immediate economic and social rewards and to take a place in society as a responsible citizen and yet not be able to influence its course in any direct manner.

The adolescent's difficulties are, then, enhanced by the contradictory and complex demands and perceptions of society at large which do not necessarily fit with the adolescent's concept of himself. In Western Society the adolescent seems to some extent to represent the repository of the projections of the cultural environment. In a culture which tends to be hypermoralistic and somewhat hypocritical about its own use of aggression, all adolescents are loosely considered to be licentious and delinquent. Yet when adolescents do behave in an aggressive or hypersexual manner, adults appear to gain vicarious satisfaction from this. Riots by gangs of youths on beaches are watched in fascinated horror by adult groups who seem almost unwittingly to obstruct the efforts of police forces to control them.

There are, however, advantages as well as disadvantages in the confused attitudes of society at large. Well institutionalized patterns for the adolescent relieve anxiety but do not allow for the ultimate production of a flexible personality.

The end of adolescence comes with the completion of certain vital social tasks. The adolescent, if he lives in a mobile society, has to cope with separation from parents, siblings and childhood friends. Anyway he must become psychologically autonomous. This autonomy, whether or not it is associated with physical separation from the original family group, should carry with it the capacity to make decisions, to regulate one's own behaviour and to assume responsibility for oneself. The parents now are there to be loved but not depended upon. Finally, the adolescent has to deal with new intellectual and economic challenges. The effectiveness with which these tasks are accomplished and the emotional cost of completing them is a measure of successful growth through adolescence.

Ability

KENNETH LOVELL

19 NOVEMBER 1964

By adolescence the individual has had a dozen years or more of interaction with his environment, and these years are of importance in determining his abilities displayed at school or work.

It has long been known that differences in the general quality of the central nervous system seem likely to be a major cause of the variation in intellectual abilities between individuals, that is, in their capacity for co-ordinating complex actions carried out in the mind. But it is now known that other influences are also important. Children who receive parental encouragement, or experience good teaching and a stimulating environment, or children who are emotionally stable or whose thoughts are not too greatly disturbed by fantasy, are all likely to develop greater abilities than would otherwise be the case, since they tend to build up over the years a mental organization that is richer and more flexible. Moreover, emotional stability, introversion and persistence (which is linked with introversion) all influence, even before adolescence, the degree to which young people can steadfastly apply their abilities to school and other work, thereby affecting school attainment and work performance.

To about 12 years of age a child's thoughts are closely tied to concrete situations in his immediate experience. But from 12 onwards, new and important thinking skills begin to emerge. Due to his continuing interaction with the social *milieu* and the maturation of the central nervous system, the adolescent can increasingly elaborate more complex expectancies when faced with certain kinds of data. His logical thought now extends to statements or propositions relating to objects and their properties. To illustrate this point suppose that a pupil is presented with a length of string suspended from a hook, and that one of several weights can be attached to the lower end. The subject is asked to establish what determines the period of oscillation of this simple pendulum. He can change the attached weight, vary the length of the string, alter the height from which the "bob" is released and the impetus, if any, he imparts to it initially. The adolescent can reason that *if* some particular variable (e.g. length of string) affects the time of swing, then the effect will appear *if* he holds the other variables constant and varies only the one he is considering. On the other hand, if he decides on, say, weight as the crucial influence, and carried out a corresponding procedure and found no effect on the time of swing, then he must rule out weight alone as a factor.

In essence the pupil has to consider the *merely* possible, work out the consequences if the hypothesis is true, and then verify or infirm the consequences. These new skills become available at what Piaget called the stage of *formal thought*. They become increasingly available to the secondary school pupil in mathematics, science, history, literature, etc. But for reasons not well understood, formal thought does not develop in all areas or in all situations simultaneously.

The adolescent can now build a new kind of concept, for he is no longer confined to those that are constructed out of immediate reality. He can increasingly co-ordinate relationships between concepts already constructed and build new concepts of a higher level of abstraction. Thus the concept of *proportion* becomes available, for an analogy of the form 3:4 as 15:20 involves a relationship between the first two terms (3, 4), another between the second pair (15, 20), and the establishment of the identity relationship between these two relationships. The logical structure of such a system is exactly parallel to that of a statement of proportionality. Likewise the adolescent can combine the concepts of *mass* and *temperature* and elaborate the concept of *heat* (mass x temperature). Whereas mass and temperature are mental constructs derived directly from the environment, their product is not.

Unfortunately there are many important questions relating to the growth of formal thought that cannot yet be answered. For example, what percentage of adolescents reach this stage of thinking? Can the onset of such thought be speeded up by suitable education? Is the interaction with the social *milieu*, or the zeitgeist, all important? What part does language play? Only future research can answer these questions. If, however, the thinking skills demanded of the adolescent are too far ahead of those available to him, he will assimilate, with distortion, what he is taught, and there will be no transfer to similar situations. But it does seem likely that one of the reasons that adolescents are argumentative and in verbal rebellion against adult standards, is that for the first time they can reflect on their own thoughts and feelings, hypothesize, and see that the way in which adults run the world is one of a number of possible ways.

BREAKDOWN OF ABILITY

If to a group of, say, 14 year olds of varying scholastic attainments a series of tasks is given involving words and the meaning of words, mechanical and problem arithmetic, the imaginative manipulation of shapes, and mechanical knowledge, the variation in the performance among the pupils can be accounted for by positing one main, and two group abilities.

The general ability, called g by Spearman, contributes something to all the tests. It is a matter of grasping relationships and is most strongly in evidence in the more complex intellectual tasks like reasoning or abstraction. One group ability is a verbal-numerical-educational or v:ed ability; the other the practical-mechanical-spatial or k:m ability. The former indicates the ability to understand both written and spoken words and to benefit from a verbal type of education. The latter divides into: (*a*) spatial ability or the capacity to perceive and retain mentally an impression of the form of a shape or pattern as a whole and (*b*) mechanical ability which depends on knowledge and experience of mechanical apparatus and operations. Physical abilities like speed of running, and abilities involved in manual dexterities, e.g. speed of screwing nuts on bolts, correlate with the k:m ability to some extent, but they are largely specific to the tasks involved.

Both group abilities depend upon inborn potential and cultural opportunities, and are linked to temperament. The k:m ability is in evidence by 11 years of age, but in our society is less well developed in girls than in boys. This may be partly due to the different kinds of activities in which the sexes engage from the early years. However, g would account for some 40 per cent, and the two group abilities for some 15-20 per cent, of the variability in the performance of given tasks.

The longer the training required for a particular job and the more complex the activities involved in it, the higher the level of abilities generally needed. Thus an adolescent wanting to enter a profession must obtain fairly high scores on the general and verbal-educational abilities. With more modest scores, but still above average, he is likely to be suitable for a variety of occupations ranging from salesman to toolmaker; while if his scores are average or a little below he may well be successful as a skilled craftsman such as electrician or plumber. Semi-skilled and unskilled workers score lower. Within any occupation, however, there is a great range of ability, so that some toolmakers will score higher than some accountants.

Spatial-mechanical ability is of more limited value in predicting scholastic performance, and its chief value lies in predicting competence in employment. For example, spatial-mechanical ability contributes (together with general ability) to performance in watch repairing; also to the competence of architects, civil and mechanical engineers, and draughtsmen. On the other hand the ability contributes little to one's performance as a lawyer, clerk, salesman or poultry farmer.

Between 15 and 18 there are differential changes in abilities. Vernon adduced strong evidence that general ability grows only as long as educational or other stimulus occurs. While intelligence test scores continue to rise to 25 years of age or more in students, maximum scores are reached at 15 by those who have no further education. Vocabulary size increases beyond 18, although ability to do arithmetic remains stationary for a few years after 15 or declines somewhat, unless stimulated by further schooling or work. The k:m ability increases up to the late teens.

This conceptual framework for the structure of abilities is widely accepted by British psychologists. But Eysenck and White have indicated that recent work among 15–16 year olds suggests that in emotionally labile adolescents, abilities are less clearly structured. Greater emotional stability and ability, respectively, may go with greater degrees of organization of ability and stability. Further, it must be stressed that the g, v:ed and k:m abilities are not identical with the degree and speed of learning new skills, although there is a positive correlation with these abilities in complex learning tasks. Indeed, there is little evidence that there is a general learning ability common to a wide variety of tasks—psychomotor, mechanical, verbal and non-verbal, rote and meaningful.

Those giving educational and vocational guidance to adolescents rightly attempt to assess their intellectual abilities and educational attainments. After this, their success is likely to depend mainly on how well they can assess the adolescent's relevant experience, personality traits, interests and general motivation; and then attempt to assess his specific attitudes to the type of education or job under consideration.

2
Adolescent Values
E M and M EPPEL

28 MARCH 1963

Author's note

This article is based on material forming part of "An Analysis of
the Climate of Opinion"—the preliminary phase of an investigation
into "The Moral Codes and Sentiments of Young People", undertaken for The Youth Studies and Research Foundation by E. M. and M.
Eppel. A full account of the first, on adult attitudes, part of the
investigation appeared under the title: "Connotations of Morality" in
the September 1962 number of the *British Journal of Sociology*. The
main enquiry with adolescents has involved a variety of indirect
approaches including projective devices.

The subjects of this investigation were working adolescents aged
15–18, boys and girls. Most had left school at 15, and all were attending
compulsory day-release classes in London. A variety of approaches was
adopted comprising five test situations, mostly projective, and some
discussions. The study was carried out for the Youth Studies and
Research Foundation and the Van Leer Trust.

> *A big mistake is made by trying to judge today's younger generation
> on the moral standards of yesterday. . . . They will in time set their
> own moral standards.*—Male Youth Leader.
> *Young people will be the same as the older generation when they
> get older.*—Sixteen year old junior postman.

No shortage of research exists into the behaviour of young people in our society. In fact a considerable literature is available on their patterns of spending, their leisure habits and their vocational aspirations. They are in some danger of becoming the most documented and discussed section of the community, with the consequence that some young people are showing signs of an excessive self-consciousness about their role as members of a curious, disturbing and unpredictable subspecies.

One of the areas which has been more subject to opinion than research is the moral values and sentiments of normal young people, especially young working people. The amount of factual information on this somewhat explosive subject seems to be almost in inverse proportion to the number of confident assertions, *ex cathedra* utterances and dogmatic prognostications that people are prepared to indulge in.

THE ADULT VIEW

There would seem, therefore, to be justification for some enquiry into what adults mean when they use such phrases as "the morals of adolescents" and in particular what groups of adults in positions of authority and influence mean by them, since this is likely to affect not only the public image of the adolescent, but ultimately even his image of himself. There is even more justification for an attempt to gain insight into the codes and moral sentiments of young people in our own society. A fairly extensive pilot study dealing with both these issues has been undertaken by the writer and his wife.

As a preliminary enquiry we tried to elucidate more precisely the meanings of the terms "moral" and "morality" among responsible adults in direct contact with young people, and to assess the main moral qualities they regard as important. The two investigations attempt to present a picture of some of the standards, values, and conflicts of young people through both ends of the telescope—the adult and the adolescent. To obtain information on how young people's behaviour is seen through the eyes of some adults in positions of authority a questionnaire was sent to London Juvenile Court magistrates, probation officers, and youth leaders, inviting them to express their views on the values and standards of young people in contemporary society.

The replies represent about one quarter of the total group (completed questionnaires were received from 20 Juvenile Court magistrates,

35 probation officers, and 80 youth leaders—a total of 135). They range from a few brief and categorical sentences indicating unqualified views to elaborate documents of 1,000 words and more. About 40 per cent of the replies were from adults concerned primarily with delinquent youths and 60 per cent from those concerned with non delinquents.

The concept of "moral" and morality clearly had different connotations for different subjects, but our main categories of interpretation emerge. There is also evidence of two broad standpoints: one stressing the positive elements of morality—for example, duty, obligation, responsibility, and one stressing the negative aspects—for example, restraint, inhibition and conformity.

The analysis of the climate of opinion had shown that discussions of adolescent morals have been dominated by consideration of their sexual behaviour. However, only five of the subjects adopted an exclusively sexual interpretation of moral in this investigation.

INTERPRETATION OF "MORAL"

	No. of subjects	%
Predominantly *Sexual*	5	3·5
Predominantly *Religious*	30	22
Predominantly *Social/Humanitarian*	85	63
Predominantly *Rational/Psychological*	10	7·5
Unclassifiable	(5)	–

Some of those who replied clearly had deep religious convictions that shape their attitudes to morality. This constituted the second largest group of the respondents, but only about 22 per cent. In some cases all the answers were directly related to the standpoints, sanctions and codes of Christianity; in others there were indirect comments on the importance of religion and of a sense of "spiritual values" and of the willingness to accept a code dictated by religion.

I think they should be encouraged to mix with Christian people and study, as far as possible, the Christian faith in order that they may have an opportunity to decide what life is all about and find a purpose for their lives apart from the amassing of too many material possessions. In other words to get life into perspective and learn the things of real value. . . . Keeping them if possible within a Church Fellowship. . . .

The *social humanitarian* interpretation of morality constitutes by far the largest group, and is given by 63 per cent of the subjects. The dominant consideration with these people is that morality is subsumed in obligation to the community, the duties of citizenship and service, and in the realization that "people matter". A fairly wide range of specific humanitarian criteria are invoked by this group. These tend to be of differing degrees of comprehensiveness and complexity but prominent among them are such concepts as justice, considerateness, courtesy and respect for the rights of others. The following are typical responses:

A sense of responsibility to the community in which they live (indirectly), to the wider community, and to themselves. This will affect their relationships with people in all spheres. An understanding of the real potentialities of life for every individual.

I do not look for specific moral characteristics, but rather for a personality that tends to treat people as people, rather than people as "things" (to be used).

Finally a small group (ten subjects) adopt a *rational psychological* interpretation of moral.

Initially an awareness of the reality of that field of morals which is codified in laws. More broadly to encourage the making of judgments about behaviour which can facilitate worthwhile relationships.

. . . the capacity to make their own decisions and think for themselves is the main quality to be encouraged amongst the young.

An individual honesty, so that he/she may reject and oppose those things in modern society that although accepted are not moral. Above all the moral qualities of the searcher and fighter for those things he as an individual holds to be true.

Although for most of the subjects the concept "moral" is clearly highly complex, for others it is simple and reducible to a single principle. What is striking however is that the majority are clearly concerned with social/humanitarian considerations and sanctions. This finding is further reinforced by an analysis of the specifically mentioned virtues.

	Frequency of Reference
Social obligations, consideration for people	145
Honesty, truthfulness, sincerity, integrity	73
Thrift, industry, respect for property	29
Independence of thought, judgment	20
Respect for authority, age, dependence on Divinity	17

DIFFERENCES BETWEEN THE GENERATIONS

It is clear that whether or not their views have any sound basis in objective fact, the picture that these adults in positions of authority have of the differences between the generations will have an effect on their attitudes to young people and on the image held by the general public. Some subjects mention more than one area of difference, but about half comment on changes in sexual behaviour and attitudes and believe that the changes in this sphere are both obvious and substantial. There is considerable agreement among them that sex activity plays a bigger part in the lives of young people than it did in the previous generation, or at any rate it is indulged in more openly and is discussed more freely.

PRIMARY GROUP INFLUENCES

	Total References
Parents/Family	69
Teachers	21
Other Adults	44
Own Generation	18
Total	**152**

SOCIETY AND ITS VALUES

	Total References
Mass Media and Materialism	77
Commercialism	45
Religion	34
World Situation	10
Total	**166**

Generally those who commented on this disapprove of it, but a number either reserve their judgment or indicate that there may be some positive as well as negative features to be considered. Only two subjects believe that the atmosphere is healthier and saner in sex matters than it was in their generation.

There are hints by some of the subjects that there may be a tendency to interpret the behaviour of people from one social class or tradition in terms of the norms appropriate to another:

> ... in my youth sex was in the cupboard, now it is on the breakfast table.

> ... in their sex relationships, where casual intimacy tends to be taken much more for granted not only in cases where feelings of affection exist, but in cases where there is only attraction. Chastity is a hardly understood virtue.

> Sexual morals are neither better nor worse—just different and nearer the early 19th than the early 20th century.

The second largest number of references (39 per cent) was to changes in discipline and attitudes to authority. The majority of these references stress disapproval of the change. A smaller proportion record the change but are disinclined to commit themselves to judgments about them. Two subjects are clear that the change is substantial and approve of it mainly on the grounds that it gives greater opportunity for the development of self-discipline and autonomy of conscience.

> There has been a general breakdown of discipline and a sense of authority, and this has extended to all areas of life.

> It is not untrue to say that Juvenile Court magistrates are often laughed at, and do more harm than good by "reasoning" with offenders instead of firmer disciplinary measures.

> Condoning of wilful wrong by a tolerance out of all proportion ... the general weakening of the authority of both Church and State.

> The teenager of 20 and 30 years ago was to some extent disciplined by a great deal more parental control, religious taboos 'or genuine faith' ... but there is more freedom and opportunity to become a complete person today than ever before—welfare state infinitely more Christian than benevolent capitalism.

From my experience on the Juvenile Bench, that is, of young people of whom I have no previous private or personal knowledge, I should say that they have less respect for parental authority than we had (and often with reasonable cause) and are much more frank —but not necessarily defiant—in their claims for independence.

Whether we like it or not, the days of paternalism are ended. Modern young people, I find, will not accept or respond to any "authority" of the "because I say so" kind.

A number of reasons are adduced by some of those disapproving of the trend to account for its impetus. Prominent among these are what are seen to be the effect of modern child rearing practices derived from psychological theory, and modern methods in education. The common factor apparently is the degree of permissiveness characteristic of these practices, which is seen by most as deleterious. A small minority refer to its potentially liberating implications.

The third area of changed behaviour and attitudes on which there is substantial agreement by these subjects elicits a different orientation of attitudes—36 per cent refer to evidence of greater frankness and intellectual honesty, more open discussion and criticism of conventional codes, and a search for personal standards. The general view seems to be that young people today are less hypocritical.

Young people are certainly more open about immorality . . . if honesty in this respect can be deemed virtuous?

The modern youngster has in some ways a more transparent honesty, if only to be hollowness of life as he knows it. There is no longer the shabby pretence that once prevailed.

There seems to be more real thought about the standards they adopt, and less tendency to accept other people's standards without testing their validity.

INFLUENCES ON THE YOUNG

Among the most controversial issues is that which concerns the major influences on the moral standards of young people. Clearly anything approaching an adequate answer must include a variety of psychological and sociological considerations. It was therefore thought important to canvass the views of this group of adults in positions of authority, since they are likely to oppose those influences they regard as unsatisfactory, and support those that are seen to be constructive. The influences mentioned fall into two major categories as indicated in the table.

Most of the comments on these influences are critical or even hostile, with only a small number discussing both the good and bad aspects. Although the importance of home background is referred to more often than any other influence arising from personal relationships it is mentioned by only about half the subjects.

There are also many references to the influence of the *general values* current in contemporary society, and in particular to the ways these are reflected in and disseminated by the mass media. In fact the mass media are specifically mentioned by 77 subjects who tend to emphasize their deleterious influences. Attention is also drawn to what is seen to be a general preoccupation with material prosperity and the commercial exploitation and stimulation of human needs.

> Too often the symbols of success for youth are measured in acquisitions . . . the mainspring of Western culture.

> Overshadowing everything, there is the drab glitter of our futile "Affluent Society".

> The Younger Generation are subjected to such "high power" salesmanship on every aspect of living, that in my opinion it's no wonder that their moral codes are affected.

A small number of these adults in positions of authority who discuss what they think must be done, stress the danger of insisting too much on conformity and believe that what is most important is to provide the conditions that will foster a capacity for reflection and discriminating judgment.

> More and more responsibility and recognition must be passed to the youngster much earlier. There must also be much less mealy mouthedness. . . . One of the more exciting things I have discovered is the readiness to serve on the part of youngsters if they are allowed to devise ways of service for themselves.

> I do not believe morals should be passed on in the form of formal teaching as this is the very atmosphere which kills a young person's ability to decide, judge and pursue a line of healthy moral attainment.

Most of the time, both with this group and generally, the emphasis has been on the need for adults to understand the problems of young people, but one subject makes the interesting point that it may be equally important to help young people to understand adults (a number of the young people in this enquiry seem to feel the same).

They are virtually made a race apart... and they are not so helped to take their place with adults... is enough done about helping young people to understand adults which is one of the biggest problems?

The current adult image of the adolescent generation then is a somewhat melancholy one, compounded of many simples, but prominent among them is the view that there has been a marked decline in respect for authority. But what about the other side of the coin?

THE YOUNG VIEW

Indications of the attitudes to authority of the 230 working adolescents who were the subjects of a second research project were given at many places in the battery of test situations and in some of the discussions. Occasionally they arose at unforeseen places, or were offered gratuitously, which is perhaps an indication of the extent to which the nature and expression of authority concerns these young people. These attitudes were specifically explored in some detail at various points in this study, for the most part by providing partly structured stimuli that would invite reactions derived from their experiences of, and feelings about authority. Characteristic of these was an item in the unfinished sentences test, "When people give orders..." It is clear from the nature of their responses that their frame of reference is mainly the work situation. The table below summarizes the responses of the 212 subjects completing this item.

WHEN PEOPLE GIVE ORDERS...

		Boys	Girls	Total	
Accept	unconditionally	11	16	27	131
	conditionally	44	60	104	
Reject	conditionally	19	9	28	81
	unconditionally	31	22	53	
	Total	105	107		

The following examples are characteristic of the minority (12 per cent) who say they would accept orders unconditionally.

You must do as they say.

You should obey them even if you don't agree with them.
I take them because I know that at one time or another they had to take orders.

The biggest group, about 50 per cent, are those who say they would accept conditionally:

If I think they are right I obey, as long as no hardship is caused to others.

They should be thought about and then carried out if they are reasonable.

They should make sure they are right.

They should stick to them, not keep changing their mind.

They should not do so as though they own the place. If orders are given nicely—"Obey them".

. . . carried out better if they were given in a humane way.

They should do it in a proper way and not shout at you.

The considerations that weigh with those who reject conditionally, about 13 per cent, are often very similar to those in the previous group, but the stress is rather more negative.

It might be their duty, but otherwise they would not get away with anything with me.

I resent it if they give them in an unfriendly way.

I resent it if the orders are given by someone I dislike.

I don't like taking them. If people ask me I do it for them.

The last group, 25 per cent, are those who express themselves as uncompromisingly hostile to the authority latent in the idea of people who give orders.

I'd like to tell them to pipe down.

They should be punched and they themselves given orders.

It makes me feel mad, they show off because they have a high grade.

It makes me sick, they are the big high and mighty, whom if we try to reason with them we are called louts.

I try to resist because I do not like being ordered around.

When one looks more closely at the kind of conditions which are stressed by these young workers, it is clear that there is a considerable concern for good human relations and a resentment of authoritarianism. The dominant attitude is summed up in the declaration of one 17 year old: "They should put themselves in the place of the person to whom they give the order. . . . An order can be made into a friendly gesture by asking a person to do something."

Closely related to the personal and moral problems that are involved in attitudes to authority are those that arise from the desire to achieve independence. The drive to attain adult status is regarded as a ubiquitous feature of patterns of adolescence in the Western world.

Once again the evidence for general inferences is derived from a number of areas of the research, but some of the main conflicts and difficulties are placed in focus by the responses to another item in the unfinished sentences test, "If you stand up for yourself . . ." Two hundred of the subjects completed this item.

If You Stand Up for Yourself . . .

	Boys	Girls	Total
Unqualified Approval	55	70	125
Qualified Approval	5	10	15
Difficulties emphasized	40	20	60
Total	**100**	**100**	**200**

It is noticeable that the boys are inclined to stress the difficulties more than the girls, and to be more acutely concerned with adult criticisms and threats to their independence. This may to some extent reflect the greater difficulties that these boys actually experience in their relations with the adult world, especially at work, or a greater drive on

their part to assert themselves against adults. Throughout this research there is clear evidence that this group of young people feels itself to be unjustly and sweepingly criticized by a hostile or indifferent adult generation that takes little trouble to understand their problems, and often misinterprets their behaviour to an extent that makes them feel hopeless and frustrated.

I think we should stand up for ourselves. Especially against these older people who think they are better than us.

You will find that people will respect you and you will find more friends.

It is better because other people won't walk over you.

You are a much better person than someone who takes every insult.

You should always keep to your own point of view and never be swayed by others.

People won't take advantage of you and you will be respected.

You shouldn't be cheeky, just say what you think is right. And admit when you're wrong.

Sometimes it is wrong and sometimes not, depending on who is right.

You should also stand up for other people.

But perhaps the most illuminating commentary is provided by the 30 per cent who dealt with the difficulties and consequences of standing up for themselves:

As a rule you get pushed down again by parents and teachers. . . .

Someone always says that you are being impertinent.

When I believe I am right I will argue it out, but older people just think I am being cheeky.

You are called insolent by the older generation, yet if you say nothing, you are a coward or chicken.

You're a yob you would get a belt in ear from a oldey.

It is important to realize that, rightly or wrongly, this is the picture that a substantial proportion of these ordinary young working people have of adult reactions to their wish to assert independence. Since most of them regard this wish as natural, worthy of approval, and morally sound, adults ought to understand the extent to which they think that it is being blocked.

These comments illustrate some of the difficulties this group of young working people feel stand in the way of the expression of their individuality. A picture of ego ideals and of the frustrations that they may suffer in attempts to realize them is provided from a number of sources in this enquiry, including an essay, and their responses to a moral beliefs test, but once again some of the most striking material can be derived from their reactions to another of the unfinished sentences. The sentence beginning, "I deserve praise when . . ." was included because it seemed likely to provide an oblique indication of the moral qualities they regard as most important and also because studies in developmental and industrial psychology have stressed the importance of some approval and praise as a positive incentive to effort. How far is the wish for praise and approval part of the tissue of expectation of these young people, and how far are they likely to see it satisfied? The following table provides a summary of their reactions:

I Deserve Praise When . . .

	Boys	Girls	Total
Conformity to accepted codes	54	73	127
Social/Humanitarian	21	24	45
Expectations of praise	12	6	18
Miscellaneous (e.g. getting married)	6	2	8
Total	**93**	**105**	**198**

The girls tended to be somewhat more articulate than the boys in their response to this item and to particularize a little more freely. The majority of both sexes felt they should be praised for conformity to conventional codes of good behaviour (a few for keeping out of trouble and exercising self-control) or for attempting to achieve some form of excellence, usually unspecified. Their somewhat generalized responses are illustrated thus,

I deserve praise when . . . :

I am a good girl.

I haven't done anything wrong at home for more than a week.

I do something outstanding.

I do that that is not expected of me. When I do it well.

In mine and other people's opinion I have done a good job.

I manage to keep my temper when arguing with an adult.

I do something which is worthwhile.

The next largest group, about one in four, give a more specifically social/humanitarian interpretation in their response to this item. In this they are in accord with the opinion of the adults.

I have done something really well and it is a help to the community.

I do something for the mentally handicapped, the blind, polio victims, etc., etc.

When I do something extremely good for the benefit of someone else.

Idiotic men are moaning at my mates and I stand up for them.

Embedded in the responses of many in the first two categories are indications that they regard praise as unusual, rare, and awarded only for outstanding or exceptional achievements—no doubt an interesting reflection of their experience. A number however give explicit indications of the extent to which praise is or is not part of their lives:

I don't do nothing good to be praised for.

I don't get any at all.

Never unless I ask for it.

Finally, it is clear that some young people feel they deserve more praise than they receive:

I deserve praise when I do something that is worth a bit of praise. But people do not often praise teenagers nowadays.

Sometimes I go to a lot of trouble to do good. They do not even say "Thank you".

Another way of gaining insight into the picture of ego ideals is to consider those aspects of behaviour that are regarded as wrong—100 boys and 100 girls completed the sentence beginning, "It's wrong to . . ." mentioning 250 items, and although it is difficult to estimate the extent to which these conscious or avowed beliefs may influence their actual behaviour, it is clear that some interesting light is thrown on what they consider to be morally reprehensible. The value of these responses once again lies in their salience, that is, the extent to which they are produced without prompting. The following table is a summary of the things considered wrong:

THINGS CONSIDERED WRONG

	Boys	Girls	Total
Unfairness to people	36	30	66
Violence	29	31	60
Law breaking	21	20	41
Disobeying authority of elders	14	7	21
Premarital sex relations	8	12	20
Dishonesty	16	—	16
Lack of integrity	6	7	13
Miscellaneous—drink, smoke, lazy	5	8	13
Total	**135**	**115**	**250**

Several spontaneous comments show how difficult they feel it may be to live up to their beliefs, or how there may be mitigating circumstances. The largest single group is concerned for good human relations and is sensitive to all forms of personal injustice, unfair criticism, intolerance or selfishness. When to these references are added those of condemning cruelty and violence of all kinds, it can be seen that social/humanitarian values lie at the core of their moral codes, as they did for the representatives of the adult generation discussed earlier. Here, too, there is substantial backing for law and order as for honesty and integrity. There are some indications that their main preoccupation is by no means with chastity, although in several places in this research they deny that they are promiscuous and irresponsible. "It's wrong to think that teenagers are a lot of sex starved people." The following examples give some insight into their concept of wrong doing.

do everything; according to old people you can't do anything.

talk bad about people you know nothing about.

judge people by what others say.

to accuse somebody of something before you have any proof.

to victimize before knowing the facts, i.e. unmarried mothers.

to criticize people and say they are wrong because they may be right.

It is worth stressing that the main preoccupation of these young people is to use the quality of personal relations rather than accepted authority as the basis for judging what is "wrong" in behaviour.

It is interesting to turn from this picture of some of the pressures and moral conflicts that beset these young people to the methods they say they would employ to deal with them. The reactions of this group to the phrase "When I am in trouble . . ." provide some useful data. The term trouble seems for the most part to be interpreted by the boys as implying conflict with authority, or lawbreaking. For the girls it clearly involves more private considerations, often sexual in character, and implying shame or disgrace. The underlying assumption with the majority is that trouble is their own fault. Their responses are summarized thus:

WHEN I'M IN TROUBLE . . .

	Boys	Girls	Total
Seek help from family	34	24	58
Seek help from other adults	15	10	25
Seek help from friends	11	12	23
Pray to God	3	—	3
Take individual responsibility	25	38	63
Expect punishment, not help	13	14	27
Never in trouble	3	6	9
Emotional reactions only	5	11	16
Total	**110**	**114**	**224**

The largest group, over 50 per cent, say they would seek help when in trouble. Of these the majority would turn to some members of their families and believe they would meet with a helpful response. It is worth noting how many stress that they are lucky in that not all families would understand or sympathize. A few would like to turn to parents but are dubious about their reactions.

I can usually go to my parents and they will do the best they can for me without a gigantic argument as some people cannot.

I like to think that my parents are still on my side through thick and thin.

I would be very upset if my parents and relations didn't stand by me.

I always turn to my mother and father for help, as I know that they will always help me.

talk about with my mother. Before my father died I would not do so as my father would not listen to anybody else's opinion.

I ask advice from either my mother or father or if that trouble is secret, my grandfather.

You look for your parents for help and most of them don't want to know, because of what the neighbours will say.

A number would look to adults outside the family and hope to benefit from their experience, wisdom and detachment.

I go to the person who understands the subject which is troubling me.

I tell a complete stranger and then go away happy.

I would seek the advice of somebody older and a little bit wiser than myself.

A substantial proportion of these adolescents, 40 per cent, make it quite clear that they would accept personal responsibility for dealing with trouble and do not expect or desire assistance from anyone, some even expecting punishment. Rather more boys than girls are represented in this group—a reversal of the pattern for those who would seek help. A variety of reasons for self-reliance, and of strategies for dealing with the problem are advanced:

I don't trust no one.

I get myself out of it by myself.

I try to get myself out of it before I take it to anybody else, so I know what I am doing.

I keep it to myself, unless it's really bad.

I like to get over it without involving unnecessary persons.

A small number confine their responses to a description of their emotional reactions to the experience of being in trouble. These vary from extreme forms of self-reproach and shame to equally extreme forms of physical action and aggression.

I get a funny feeling in my stomach and feel very shameful.

I get very scared and nervy and hate everyone and everything.

I like to get drunk and forget about it.

I feel like hitting all the coppers I see.

The picture that is emerging of this group of young working people is that they regard themselves as members of a generation severely handicapped by distorted stereotypes about their behaviour and moral standards. Many of them feel this so acutely that they believe that whatever goodwill they manifest is at best not likely to be appreciated, and at worst may be misinterpreted to their disadvantage. They see themselves in a good light—not as saints but as better than the sinners they believe most adults think them.

Arising from this is a considerable disenchantment with adults, particularly with those in positions of authority. There is, however, no generalized hostility to authority, rather a disinclination to accept it without question, and a strongly expressed view that it might be exercised by adults with more concern for their feelings, and for good human relations generally. Indeed the quality of personal relations seems to be the main touchstone for their assessment of their own and others' moral standards.

They are able to advance a number of criteria for good personal relations, and it is clear that though a small minority are prejudiced, for example, against coloured immigrants, most believe that what makes for harmony and tolerance is good, and that what makes for disruption and discrimination is bad. They are also acutely conscious of the difficulties in living up to their ideals, and of the extent to which many of them fall short of what they might expect of themselves. There is much that points to a genuine, if confused, concern with moral problems and moral conflict.

Finally, it is worth noting that although only a few of the adults in the earlier enquiry commented spontaneously on the possible influence of world insecurity and the threat of atomic warfare on young people, many of the young people themselves do. No questions were asked about this, nor was there any prompting, but at various relevant (and even apparently irrelevant) points a considerable number of these young people seize the opportunity to say something about this issue, often accompanying their forcible comments with drawings of mushroom clouds and CND badges. Reference to world insecurity and the atom bomb are made gratuitously by 40 per cent of these adolescents, often several times each.

One morning to pick up the paper and find nothing about war or bombs.

It's wrong to prepare for nuclear war. I am *too young to die*.

It's wrong to hate. If there was not hate they'd be no war or bombs.

It's hard to grow up in a world threatened by atomic war without wanting to do a lot and live and dress slightly unorthodoxly.

A lot of people are in favour of atom bomb testing, yet when a bomb is exploded they make no fuss at all.

Very soon, if a few stupid men do not watch out it will be the end of the world.

Young people like to enjoy life while they can, with the threat of the H bomb over their heads.

It isn't fair to experiment with nuclear weapons for distructing the world.

I would try to make a peaceful world for the next generation.

I would get rid of the bomb and live a quiet life.

3
Teenage Values
E M and M EPPEL

14 NOVEMBER 1963

As you can see, I can be like this person if I really try....
16 year old boy.

In the current heated discussions on the morality of adolescents many views are proffered on what are seen to be the most potent influences in the development of young people's values. The range of suggested influences is wide, comprehending the "materialism" manifested by the mass media, family standards, and peer group pressures; prominent too is the suggestion that the characteristics of pop idols are greatly admired and emulated, with the result not merely of bizarre behaviour but of frustration arising from an unrealistic view of life and a straining after the unlikely. Very little factual information is available on just how strong these influences are and how they operate—a circumstance that may vitiate the debates, but seldom reduces their temperature.

One way of gaining some insight into this problem is to try to find out the sort of people used as models by adolescents, on the hypothesis that strong sentiments for people are likely to be or to become sentiments for what the people believe in or stand for. If a reasonably comprehensive picture of the model is provided then useful data on aspirations, values, and admired personality characteristics may be made available. The authors elicited information on the models of groups of young working people of both sexes (15-18 years) in London

35

as part of a study of moral codes and sentiments. At various points in the research there are indications given of models and aspirations, but the most direct data are contained in essays written on the theme "The person I would most like to be like".

TO BE MYSELF

The most striking impression gained from the analysis of these essays is of the substantial proportion who declare they have no wish to be like anyone other than themselves. Approximately half the girls (52 per cent) and more than one third of the boys (37 per cent) state specifically that they enjoy their lives and are happy and contented. "I would just like to be myself." Some suggest minor modifications they would welcome in their personalities or life circumstances, but 25 boys and 42 girls are content to be themselves without qualification. The following are examples of these sentiments:

Girls

I would just like to be ME! So far I have had a very happy life.

I'm glad I'm me. My mum and dad are the two most wonderful people in the world, although we argue. I've got two terrible brothers but I love them enough to put up with their pranks and arguing.

I like being myself. I'm quite content with life really. I have brothers and sisters, a mother and father who are all very good to me. We have plenty to eat, a clean bed to sleep in. Many people throughout the world haven't got any of these good things.

I am quite happy as myself, in fact I couldn't wish for more at the moment. I have the most wonderful parents and there are people who are really worse off than I am.

I don't want to be like anyone else, I'm happy in just being myself. I'm happy at home with my family, I'm satisfied with my job and the people I work with. If you are not satisfied with what you have in life, think of the many people who are deaf and dumb or cripples, etc., and think how lucky you have been that you are not like them.

Models Chosen	Boys (115)	Girls (115)	Total (230)
Self	43	60	103
Father	1	2	3
Mother	—	4	4
Siblings	—	1	1
Uncle	1	—	1
Friends	4	8	12
Other people	66	40	106

Occupations of Models			
No change	55	50	105 (46%)
Ordinary	15	26	41 (18%)
No work at all	5	7	12 (5%)
Glamorous	35	26	61 (26%)
Altruistic	5	6	11 (5%)

Boys

I would like to be myself and nobody else at the moment. I am happy and I think that is all that matters really.

I am quite content with my own life. My life is no more nor less than any average teenager. I do an average amount of work and have an average amount of amusement. It is not a perfect life I lead but it is good enough for me.

I would not change the way I live for anythink else. I have a good job which I enjoy very much ... I am not very bright but I can understand most things which are put in front of me.

I would like to be like myself because I have no worries and I enjoy life. I am happy at my work ... and have no need for extra money as I lead a fairly happy life. I don't mind what I do. I am well liked and have plenty of friends who are all my own age.

I am quite content to be myself and do not intend to model myself on some other body. Of course I want to better myself but I never wish to do and behave like my friends. I think to be an individual if not carried too far ("No man is an island unto himself") is a great asset. ... At certain stages I am fed up with myself but in the end I am glad that I am still me!

Among those who would like to be like themselves are a number who specify modifications they would wish including such things as more money, promotion, better education, greater maturity, for example:

> I would like to be richer than I am . . . but in person I would like to stay myself.

> I would like to be a bit more wealthy. I don't think I get enough money a week and I always find that I am broke by Tuesday.

> I would much rather be myself. I would like a bit more money, but as long as I have my health and strength to work then I am satisfied.

> I would have liked to have had a better education. Also I would like security in my job and to enjoy more work to the full. I wouldn't like to actually be anyone else, I want to be the same old me but I would like to have a better job.

> I don't think I'd like to be anybody else, although I'd like to make a few changes to myself. My temper is too quick and I can be very catty if something goes wrong.

> I do not think I would wish to be anyone else but I would certainly like to change a few of my ways. For instance I get quite disturbed if asked to do something which will alter my routine greatly. Another of my faults is arguing with my Grandmother. . . .

It is clear that the majority of the subjects, and particularly those who express satisfaction with their lot in life, are firmly rooted in reality. They have "no time to dream foolish fancies", for "After all is said and done, I prefer to be ME as God created me."

The spontaneous discussion they provide of their reasons for wishing to remain themselves throws light on the things they value and on some important factors in adolescent adjustment. The vast majority of contented subjects, particularly the girls, attribute their attitude to a happy family life, sometimes with glowing praises of "the most wonderful and understanding parents in the world". A minority talk also of good friends, of both sexes. Some, especially boys, discuss their enjoyment of work and of leisure.

Very few of these "contented" adolescents present a picture of arrogance, smugness, or illusion about themselves. Many of them clearly are able to imagine a different life, but are prepared to settle for reality.

It's funny when you are asked to sit down and write an essay on who you would like to be like, you find you don't find it as good as you thought. . . . Most of all, I would like to be myself at my age now and grow up quite naturally as I hope I'm doing with lovely long eyelashes. . . . 17 year old typist.

FATHER IS PERFECT

Of the 127 subjects who wish to be like someone other than themselves, very few choose a member of their own family, only 2 boys and 7 girls (against this must be laid the number of "contented" subjects who pay tribute to parents and other members of their families). Those who evince such strong family sentiments express themselves with considerable feeling.

The person I should most like to be like is my father, because he's understanding, loving, gentle and has a great personality. My father has a very strong carractor. When he was a child his family were poor, he made up his mind his family would have everything he didn't. This he has succeeded in doing. I love and respect my father and if I could be the same as him, I should thank God. My father is not very tall, about 5 ft 7 in, is 46 and still has long jet black hair. He is extremely young in his appearance, and loves his children and his wife. He has no temper, but gets annoyed at times. . . . Now that he has educated us he's started buying household luxuries . . . and a nice home. To me my father is perfect in every way. . . . 15 year old boy.

The person I am writing about is a retired policeman who is 6 feet tall and weighs 17 stone. He has had eight children, the youngest being 18 years . . . to my eyes there couldn't be a happier family. . . . This man has not only brought his children up the right way, but he has worked all through the night for them, so that they could have little luxuries. . . . I cannot say very much about this man as I couldn't possibly do it all in the time, it would take pages and pages. As you probably guessed this man is my DAD. . . . 18 year old girl.

If I really had to choose someone, I think I would choose my mother. She is very kind and always helps any one who needs it, she is the dearest person in the world, I would like to be like her, more than anyone else.... girl of 17.

I should just like to be an ordinary person, happily married with my husband and children around me. In fact if I could be just that, then I would be my mother all over again. She is content with her life, and being her daughter, I should like to be my mother.... girl of 17.

I would like to be like my elder sister because through her life of 20 years she has had to work, but she has got somewhere. She has a very nice personality and character, with good looks. She has a very good job and a nice husband with lots of friends, and money and brains to go with it.... girl of 15.

My idol is my 40 year old uncle. My first reasons are he has a wonderful sense of honour.... Also if I like to talk to him about any subject he nearly always gives me a reasonable answer and always has time to listen.... When I am older I hope that I am at least half the man he is.... 16 year old boy.

In view of the emphasis laid by some on the importance of a teenage subculture, it is interesting to note that whereas many references are made to the wish to have lots of friends (and clearly these young people attach great importance to friendship), only 12 subjects, 4 boys, 8 girls, chose friends as their models. Sometimes the motive is admiration, sometimes it reveals a complex network of values and aspirations which are mirrored in the friends they wish to emulate.

A Good Mate

I would like to be like John. He is big and he is a good mate.... 16 year old boy.

The person I would like to be like is not anybody famous but a good friend of mine. She has a wonderful vivacious personality and a natural instinct to make you laugh. She has money and plenty of clothes, but is not spoilt. She is pretty and has a regular boy friend.... She would never cause an argument.... 16 year old girl.

She is a very pleasant girl and seldom gets annoyed or moody. She is very understanding and I can always rely on her for good advice, if I need it. Like me she is a shorthand typist.... We have been good friends now for about nine years. . . . Her parents are not rich, but decent working class people. She has almost the same interests as me. . . . 16 year old girl.

Incidentally among the personality qualities most admired in friends, and in others, especially by the girls, are vivacity, enthusiasm, and a capacity for good social relationships.

There have been many indications throughout this research of the deep interest these young people have in the quality of personal relationships. Further light is shed on this by a consideration of the sex of the models and the many incidental comments on relationships between the sexes.

While all the boys choose people of their own sex, seven of the girls choose male subjects. Two of these girls wish to be like their fathers, and one like Adam Faith, not specifically for his masculinity, but because "he has a lovely personality and lots of people like him". Four girls express a wish to belong to the opposite sex. The reasons they give throw light on possible tensions between the sexes that may arise from differential treatment and opportunity. A few boys support the view that they have more privileges as members of the male sex, for example:

> I like to be a boy. In my opinion they have an easy life and don't have to do much work in the home. Also being a boy would give more chances of meeting people, because a boy can always go up to a girl and start talking to her, but if a girl did this they would think she was cheap. . . . clerical worker, 15 years.

But the great majority of the girls and boys identify themselves with members of their own sex, sometimes expressing a wish to amend certain norms of behaviour, for example,

> One thing is that I wish it was the done thing for girls to ask boys out as well as boys ask girls out . . . writes a 15 year old machine operator.

LOVE AND MARRIAGE

About one quarter of the subjects make specific references to relations with the other sex, either in the boy/girl friend context or with reference to marriage.

The role of boy friends and girl friends is seen in various ways, for example, someone to share leisure activities, someone to trust and confide in, someone to satisfy vanity—"with a bird on my arm", and someone with whom to prove sexual prowess. The relationships outlined therefore range from the realistic idea of having "a steady" to the glamorous and extravagant involving several girl friends or boy friends and being "the centre of attraction". There are some hints of the conflicts with parents:

> I would like to be able to see my fiance as often as I like without having to tell lies about my whereabouts. . . . typist, 16 years.

> . . . Would have a nice good looking boy friend whom all the other girls envied. She'd go out a lot with him as they both liked the same sports and were good at the same thing. . . . telephonist, 15 years.

> I wouldn't like to be like any other girl I know. They're all catty and they always seem to think I'm trying to steal their boy friends, which I usually am, but of course if their boy friends really liked them they wouldn't let me take them away would they? . . . telephonist, 15 years.

> I would like a steady girl friend so that we could have a good time together. . . . 16 year old boy.

> I would like . . . to have girls falling over themselves to go out with me. I would like also to live with about 30 girls in my own house without my Mum and Dad and to be as free as the wind. . . . 16 year old boy.

From these occasional fantasies of sexual licence we may turn to those subjects (13 per cent) who discuss marriage in these essays. Two boys choose models about whose divorces they comment, offering negative views on marriage and family life, e.g. "too much worry and expense". Most of these boys visualize marriage as "settling down" with a "really decent girl" after a few years of fun or travelling abroad and seeking adventure to curb their "restlessness", usually somewhere in the mid 20s. Marriage is essentially linked with security.

Boys

> He has many girl friends, but although at 21 he has no possible thought of marriage, he thinks 25 is an ideal age. . . . 16 year old.

After I've seen as much as possible I would marry a decent girl about 22 years old and settle down to married life. . . . 17 year old.

. . . plenty of parties, plenty of women, up to the age of 25 to 30 years. Then begin to settle down with a nice wife, own house in suburbs, later on to have children. . . . 17 year old.

. . . travelling around the world . . . I think this would . . . straighten a person out, and on returning home would be able to settle down more easily. On returning, I would find a job with security, like the one I have now, get married, settle down for a peaceful married life. . . . A sort of restlessness. . . . 17 year old.

Girls

The girls who discuss marriage seem less concerned with the conflict between adventure and security than do the boys, although there are a few hints about "enjoying" themselves . . . e.g. 15 year old:

I would like to meet the right man for me and settle down and get married. I am not getting married too early so that I have not seen any life but would like to get married when I am about 21 years of age, when I consider I would have seen all the life I would like to.

On the other hand some indicate a wish for early marriage: "I would like to be 18 years old so that I could get married next year instead of in three years' time," wrote a 16 year old typist.

Some express a wish to be competent in their jobs, perhaps work part time when they first marry, but firmly reject the idea of a permanent career:

I do not want to be a career girl for the rest of my life but to have a home and family. . . . 17 year old.

. . . but when the children arrive she will be a full time housewife as she believes in a family upbringing for children. . . . 16 year old.

The picture of marriage drawn by these girls almost always includes children. Only one subject, a 15 year old girl, rejects the role of motherhood:

I would like to love children, which I know I never could. I dislike them immensely and would hate to have any of my own.

Occasionally a girl may decide to settle for marriage after glamorous fantasies, as this 15 year old typist:

> The person I would like to be like is Elvis' girl friend and be the envy of all the other girls . . . but he wouldn't have much time for me, because he would be thinking about his career most of the time. . . . But really I would like to be a happily married woman with about four children and a beautiful house with a handsome husband to love me.

The stereotype of the ideal family occurs often:

> I would like to get married when I am about 20 to a man who would love me for the rest of my life. I would hope to have four children, and I'm sure we would be very happy together. . . . 15 year old clerk.

In conclusion it appears that the expectation of being "a plain housewife" is deep rooted in these girls who discuss marriage, expressed once and for all, in a matter of fact way, by this 17 year old clerk:

> Of course I have the usual ambitions to be a wife and mother. And I expect I shall have been sorted out by then. At least I hope so.

It should be emphasized that in spite of the publicity given to teenage promiscuity and teenage marriage, only a small minority refer in these essays to sex (11 per cent) or marriage (13 per cent). These young people are not obsessed with the subject.

4

Teenage Idols

E M and M EPPEL

21 NOVEMBER 1963

An important index of the values of teenagers is the kind of occupations they select for the people they would like to be like. In a study of young working people (15–18 years) in London who wrote essays on this theme a surprisingly low number modelled themselves on unrealistic or glamorous roles in society.

Approximately 46 per cent of these subjects reveal no wish to change their jobs, although some of them show they would like "Good prospects and wages" and to be "really efficient", but with these should also be grouped those whose models follow *ordinary occupations*.

For the most part occupations in this category are within the possible, though not necessarily probable, attainment of this group of young people. A small minority have middle class connotations and may be remote from what they could achieve given their educational background. Often the occupations are specified, e.g. lorry drivers, cook, electrician, fireman, salesman, for the boys; typist (often private secretary to the boss), receptionist, housewife with part time job for the girls. A few simply say they would like to be like "an ordinary working man". In their reflections on the characteristics of these ordinary occupations there are a number of indications of the "work satisfactions" that they consider reasonable. The conditions mentioned include a fair living wage for a fair day's work, security, prospects, interesting activities, good mates, responsibility, and being trusted to do a job competently.

GLAMOROUS OCCUPATIONS

A small minority, 5 per cent, see themselves as being freed from the necessity to work for their living. Some of these merely indulge in romantic fantasies of being millionaires and the picture here is one of

Boys	Number
Sportsmen	19
Adventurers	8
Entertainers	4
Tycoons	4
Total	35

Girls	
Stars	13
Fashion	9
Adventurers	2
Air Hostess	1
Public Figure	1
Total	26

sheer pleasure and luxury; others express a wish to travel, be independent or satisfy some particular interest, such as painting.

> Enough money so that I could retire to Hawaii and spend the rest of my life lazing around doing nothing. . . . Personally I do not like work so that is my reason for wanting to be a wealthy man. . . . 16 year old boy.

> I'd like to have so much money that I wouldn't have to work every day. . . . 16 year old girl.

> If I could paint and sketch all day I would be in my element. . . . It would be nice to go to all the corners of the earth and paint and see what life is really like. . . . 16 year old girl.

Twenty-six per cent of these subjects choose as their models people with occupations that bring fame, wealth, travel and independence and power. When this and the previous group are combined it may be seen that fewer than 1 in 3 are unrealistic in their goals and wishes. In addition it could perhaps be argued that some of the glamorous occupations epitomize for these youngsters the essence of masculinity or femininity, since the boys stress success, athletic skill and adventure, and the girls beauty and approval. Outstanding sportsmen figure most prominently among the models in this category chosen by the boys (see table). Considerable details of the life styles of these admired figures are often provided as the following examples show:

Boys

The person I would like to be is Jimmy Greaves. His occupation is a footballer, his height is about 5 ft 10 in, age about 23, good appearance. At the moment he is playing for the Spurs, after getting a transfer from Milan ... for the price of £100,000. . . . He is a real good person and that is why I would like to be him. . . . 16 year old.

I would most of all like to be John Surtees, he can work wonders on two wheels ... some great features about him ... not a care in the world. He looks and acts as if he were just a beginner. . . . You see a true champion riding. . . . 15 year old.

I would like to be a scientist, the only scientist in the world that has a weapon far beyond the imagination. . . . If I was a great scientist and could invent a great weapon I would threaten the world with it and tell them that unless they dispensed with the atomic weapons in their power I would unleash it on the world. . . . 16 year old.

One of my main interests is nature study and animal life in general. So therefore the person I would most like to be is Armand Denis. His knowledge and experience in this field is unsurpassed. . . . His occupation is generally concerned with travelling to various parts of the world and photographing and studying wild animals. . . . 18 year old.

It is interesting that only four boys choose entertainers or pop idols as the people they would like to be like and in at least three of the cases the exotic picture is tempered by reasonably mundane considerations:

The person I would like to be like would be a famous singer. His age is 21, dresses smartly, a very likeable person, who spends his time entertaining other people and enjoys his work and is the idol of teenagers all over the world. With the money I earned I would go

travelling all over the world seeing places you see only in films.
After I've seen as much as possible I would marry a decent girl about
22 years old and settle down to married life. . . .

I think the person I would like to be is one of the Shadows whose
name is Hank. He always plays the guitar along with two others.
Every record they make nearly becomes top of the Hit Parade. This
Hank is in his 20s and he always wears a pair of glasses. He is not at
all handsome and he is married. . . .

The limits of extravagant fantasy are reached by the four boys who
would like to be like commercial tycoons, but even here the high
soaring fancy is occasionally brought down to earth with the introduction of realistic, if rueful, considerations:

I would like to be a millionaire like Clore or Cotton and own
chains of different stores. . . . I'd wear fine clothes and have at least
3 cars. I doubt if I would devote myself to business much as I would
find a really good manager. I would be able to travel round the
world for my holidays regardless of cost with no worries. I would
have my own airplane, yacht and country estate, where I would hold
parties for my friends and relations. I would visit all my properties
and make friends with the staff and sort out my arguments about
wages or work. . . . But alas I am not a millionaire and doubt if I'll
ever become one.

Of the girls 24 per cent say they would like to be like someone whose
occupation involves excitement, adulation, luxury, adventure or fame
with filmstars and singers at the top of the list.

Girls

The person I would most like to be is a film actress, Leslie Caron.
I think she has everything, gorgeous eyes, hair and features, also a
sweet figure and personality. . . . She is also a beautiful dancer. I have
seen her do ballet and modern acrobatics, and I have always wanted
to do ballet. . . . I should say Leslie Caron is about 27 or 28 years,
but looks nothing like her age, as her elfin looks help her to look
young and girlish. . . . I should imagine she has a very sweet nature
and kind. I should also think she wears the very latest in fashions
which I should like very much, if I had more money. . . . 17 year old.

I would like to be a great fashion designer with a glamorous fashion house in all the capitals of the world. I would design the most beautiful dress one could ever wish to see and wear. . . . I would be the best dressed woman in the world. . . . I may also invent new material and have it made in my factories. My customers would all be famous people. . . . My designs are exclusive. No copy of an article could be made. This may seem like hard work, but I would love every minute of it. . . . This is a very glamorous and romantic profession. . . . 17 year old.

I should like to be an artist . . . see all the wonderful sights of the world and draw all different races of people . . . visit all the art galleries, museums and antique shops . . . to be able to wear casual clothes without being called a beatnik. . . . I'd spend all my life painting and drawing. . . . 15 year old.

It is interesting to note that even in this small minority who would like to be someone famous or glamorous there are a number who have an awareness of reality, and claim, after a long fantasy of fame, that in the end they would settle for ordinary "happiness".

ALTRUISM AND MATERIALISM

There is in fact little evidence that these young working people, even at their most romantic, are seriously influenced by filmstars, pop heroes, or sports idols. Even when there is evidence of this kind of influence it is interesting to reflect on the extent to which these young people project on to their idols the qualities of character they consider desirable, as well as envying them their wealth, beauty, skill, or fame.

Finally there is a small group of subjects, 5 per cent, who choose as their models people whose occupation has some element of glamour, but which is predominantly altruistic in emphasis. Among the boys an ambulance driver and surgeon are included. Among the girls some profession to help others, for example, child care, nursing or veterinary surgeon is mentioned. The following examples of two girls, aged 17, give a picture of such altruistic sentiments.

I think I should like to be someone who helps others in trouble. Maybe a nurse caring for the sick, or relief helper. To give people courage, in times when all hope has gone. . . .

The person I would like to be like is the woman who . . . the whole of her life, can afford to give all her time to child care. I once read a book about a woman who devoted her life to this cause. . . . She inherited a lot of money . . . and she decided to start up homes for spastic children. . . . The most important thing was nurses volunteered to be employed by her. . . . She helped many children into normal life and that is the type of person I would like to be or help.

A major objective in analyzing these essays was to assess the values inherent in the models which the subjects set up for themselves. These are sometimes explicit, sometimes implicit, in the kinds of personalities they choose to emulate and in their impact on others. The assessment of the dominant value of each model was made independently by three judges. The picture that emerges underlines once again the fact that the predominant concern of these young people is for personal adjustment and good human relationships often linked with an attractive appearance.

It is true that about one third of the subjects made some reference to more money, for example, higher wages, bonuses, in order to afford better clothes, holidays or buy such things as motor scooters. However the number whose dominant value is clearly materialistic, for example, a wish for great wealth, to own expensive cars, houses, yachts or planes, is relatively small. In fact only 1 in 8 subjects are dominantly materialistic, and among these, the boys significantly outnumber the girls 4 to 1. Even these subjects with millionaire fantasies and strong material ambitions sometimes include "moral qualities" in their picture, for example, of generous and charitable millionaires.

I would like to be a person with lots of money so that I could go anywhere, do what I like. . . . telephonist 16 years.

The person I would most like to be is a man who lives in the West End in a luxury block of flats. He has three servants and a chauffeur who takes him out in his Rolls Royce. He is about 56 and owns a chain of stores which spread all over the country. He dresses well in all the posh clothes. At night he goes to dances. With all the other rich men at week-ends he goes golfing, bowling. He is a fair man and he is generous. . . . 16 year old boy.

Popularity, based on good physical appearance and an acceptable personality, ranks highest in the scale of values for these young people, and is the dominant value of 47 per cent of the subjects. It is of interest that a slightly higher proportion of boys than of girls are concerned for "the body beautiful". These subjects sometimes draw pictures of themselves with detailed measurements and descriptions of their good points. They see themselves as smart, well groomed, well dressed, and well built. They then list their desirable qualities, for example, "easy going with plenty of fun", "good natured", "self-confident", "pleasant character", "good looks and nice personality". The dominant value may be largely egocentric, in some cases even narcissistic, but frequently social considerations enter the picture.

The person I would like to be would have to be . . . steady and sure of himself. . . . His appearance would have to be clean and well dressed. He would be tall, sturdy and strong, with a shrewd judgment of people and football. . . . 16 year old boy.

The person I would like to be like is . . . five feet ten, weighs twelve stone and fresh complexion. His body is bulging with muscles and he is extremely fit . . . he does not dress too smartly nor too shabby. He wears three shirts a week, his shoes are always clean. . . . In his spare time he runs a keep fit class. He always makes sure he is in bed by 10 o'clock. He is up at 6 o'clock running round the block and coming back he has a cold wash and gets ready for work. . . . His hair is never too long. He doesn't smoke, he doesn't drink. . . . When he is 21 years old he would like to enter for Mr Universe Contest. . . . 17 year old boy.

I would like to be six feet two inches tall and well built but with a slim figure. Black hair and paralyzing blue eyes, size nine in shoes and wide hands and strong fingers and limbs . . . with a good character and a friendly happy appearance. . . . 17 year old boy.

There is a great deal of discussion in these essays devoted to the adjustment and personality characteristics of the models they would like to be like. These give some indication of the underlying values of the remaining 32 per cent of the subjects. The dominant values of these range through friendliness and good humour (10 per cent), responsibility and honesty (12 per cent) to co-operation and helpfulness (10 per cent). Typical examples of responses in these categories are:

The person I would most like to be like is . . . gay and very friendly . . . who . . . organizes recreations, outings, etc., kind and considerate. . . . . I have many friends that are gay and friendly, and I am quite satisfied with them and they with me. . . . . 16 year old boy.

She is . . . polite, jolly to talk with and very generous and good tempered, never holding a grudge against anyone. . . . 16 year old girl.

I think I would like a strong character and be able to stand on my own feet so that I have a responsible job. . . . 16 year old girl.

The person whom I would like to be is imaginary of course . . . he has a very independent personality. A responsible person, honest without a doubt, and frank in his ways. He is an extremely intelligent person, able to handle any difficulties with ease. . . . 16 year old boy.

The person I would like to be is a very patient person, very kind and energetic . . . he is very pleasant to work with and will help you if ever you need it. . . . 15 year old boy.

A minority of 8 per cent clearly reveal altruism and self-sacrifice as their dominant value (a further 10 per cent have these as important subsidiary social values implicit in the models which they wish to emulate). These values include a plea for equality, social justice, the brotherhood of man and an end to the threat of war and involve a general desire to make the world a happier place.

I would have liked to go into some profession which could help other people. Nowadays so many people are greedy, the more money they get the more they want. . . . You see so many people walking around the streets as if they had the world's troubles on their shoulders. In fact I wish the world would be a much happier place. This will only be when everyone stops worrying about money as it is said the love of money is the root of all evil. . . . 17 year old girl.

I'd like to . . . help or try to help everyone, help my country and the British Commonwealth, but not excluding other countries, live in peace with all mankind—no matter what his race, colour, or creed. Help my mother and family, friends and relations, help the poor—sick, and anyone who is suffering or in pain . . . and warning these leading countries, or else no man, animal, beast or any living thing on the face of the earth shall not survive the inhumanity of destruction in a further war. . . . 17 year old boy.

It may be seen that the personal values implicit in their essays give some indication of the attitudes and sentiments of these young working people. Most of them seem to value the things that all sensitive human beings value, and many are as honest about their own shortcomings, as any mature adult could wish to be. The tone of most of the essays makes it clear that not only do these young people often write with feeling and involvement, but also firmly believe that they mean what they say.

Finally the testament of a 17 year old clerical assistant, apart from being a genuine example of moral awareness, provides perhaps more than any other some valuable insights into the problems of growing up in the 1960s:

I would most like to be like a person brimming with personality, somebody who is listened to and whose ideas are appreciated. Also I would like to be different, to have unorthodox ideas (those do not include immoral ideas) because I believe the world is too full of "copy cats".

I would also like to be a little more cool headed and not so flustered in life. I would like to be a little more imaginative, try to make more use of the few talents I may possibly possess instead of wasting my life away!!

I would like to be a more faithful person—one way or the other. I admire both Kruschev and the Archbishop of Canterbury because they have found loyalty and faith even if it is to two completely different orders in life.

I would like to be a little less lazy, do things when I make up my mind to do them instead of putting off the issue until I worry myself sick over them. . . . I would like to gain a lot more confidence in life —be a little less vain. Above all I would like to be able to look back when I'm older and feel I have really done something with my life, even in some small way. However, since I've lived in London I have seen so many ill people—cripples, old people. Today my friend and I saw a crippled hunchback with a massive growth on the side of his neck. . . . This is only one example and for this reason I can only thank God for my health and strength and I hope the H bomb won't end it all.

5
The Tough and the Tender
RAY GOSLING

18 APRIL 1963

We have grown a permissive society of a neutral grey. Most of us when we hear of how Sheila is carrying on with Bob; that Jimmy's fiddling the firm; him across the road has been pulling a big job and her at the top of the street never went on to the telephone for leisure—as long as we're at a safe distance (legally)—we mind our own business. Do nothing about it. Don't think to go to the police, or organize ourselves to stop it. It doesn't affect us, and we pass it over with "it didn't ought to be" ... "good luck to them".

But then comes the crunch, and we can see she's pregnant and Bob's not around; he's been caught by the law and it's all over the papers. Then we lean on the wall, and point our finger: "She's got her deserts" ... "I knew. I seen her, drinking, night after night at the Admiral Rodney"—and Moses is back on the washing lines. We recall Exodus 20, verse 1, where God spake all those words. ...

Morally, we are more free than we have ever been from the bonds of the Ten Commandments. Yet when It happens to us, we run away from moral licence and hanker back for the Old Testament black and white.

On an average of about once a week some girl or friend/agent of the girl will come to me to say: "I'm having a baby, and I want to get rid of it. Do you know a cure, what about gin? Where can I get an abortion? Can you help me raise the money for the abortionist?" ... Forgotten is the boy she loved so much, if only for one night, that they did without the "precautions". And she not only thinks of what Mum will say, and the girls at work, but the guilt creeps back. She has sinned and wants to pay the price, do penance with danger, pain and money, with the drama of the Bible. She remembers her mother, her Gran saying, "You'll rue the day . . . you mark my words, if you carry on that way . . . the day of reckoning will come. . . ."

I'm *not* talking about the steady who has one in the oven before a marriage that will only legalize a reality; but the more casual encounter. She's in the pudding club. She loves him, but she doesn't want anything to do with him, not now. He loves her, and he thinks she'll get over not wanting him, and come back to love him. But she wants to have an abortion. She's determined. For one thing, if she's found pregnant, they'll chuck her out of college.

Listen, when she gets too big, she goes away. A doctor signs a certificate saying she's ill with mumps or something. She has the baby. Then back to college. Might even be able to do it all in the vacation. Few months later, if she still loves him, marry him. Take the baby back and all is well.

That's what I said, but she wants an abortion.

Later on, of course, she has the baby, and she loves him, and they get married and make a home. But why all the fuss, when she first finds out, all the fuss over abortion? Is it just because the college says if you're pregnant you leave?

I don't think so, for finding yourself in that predicament you've arrived at a crossroads and back comes Moses to replace the Pop Ten. Few try any "remedy". More try abortion, mostly because—"I mean, I don't want *his* kid"—and the majority have the baby, have it adopted or keep it. And nearly all vow never to return to the Town, the coffee bars, to the Crowd. Their loyalty to their mates has been shattered and they see the old Crowd as sinful—not necessarily the lover of that night, but the Crowd they were hanging around with.

You don't realize there are morals; that morals have anything to do with you until It happens; and then you want to kill yourself —you want the wrath of God to fall on you.

So, after all, find the steady boy friend and don't wait for the right one to turn up, but grab one quick, get your name down on the housing list and make the best of it all. Or disillusioned, they leave the hospital to tread the path to old maidenhood; or take up good works as a nurse; or go on the game and make yourself really cheap. Few of them keep up their vows, but at the moment of the crunch, they return to the world of black and white that is inbred and ingrained in all of us: a guilt-ridden search for punishment and a striving to do penance for the great mistake.

You beg for the justice of Moses and the Primitive Methodist Church. Like Grandma Booker of Crich who fell in love with a man in the same village in 1919. She didn't know intercourse made babies. And one night it happened. Nine months later, an alligator.

The baby daughter was taken in a cot to the railway station, and travelled down the Midland Line to Derby and to Grandma Booker's sister, a kind, now-old girl called Grandma Ottewal. There she grew up. And him—the lover of Grandma Booker—he ran away, and has never been seen, or heard of since. And she—she stayed on, alone, with her hurt and her pride in the village of Crich.

That is but one story from one naked village, when we lived with a blind, cast iron morality. Then we were in a straitjacket, and when you stepped outside you knew it was sin. You did your penance and kept your pride. Nothing permissive. And then we came, who asked for freedom and were given a washing machine, a fridge and a car— 20 down and a dollar a week till you die. We asked for sex and were offered a packet of johnnies or marriage lines, a fairy tale or a booklet of artistic poses. We asked and we were right to ask. A new working class generation arrived, dispossessed of their puritan heritage—the "free" —but what we were given wasn't the goods.

And it needs more than one generation to exorcize the blood of Grandma Booker.

In this generation there are, I think, three discernible strands—it's not as simple as that and each one of us has something from each of the strands; but I shall think of there being three.

The hard, the teddy-boy—those who go against the Ten Commandments and know it—why shouldn't they? We live in a rotten world, let's be rotten. "I broke half of them, so I thought I might as well break the rest". Morals, and they know straight away what you're talking about:

Well, thou shalt not kill—that comes first, and that's important because I often want to . . . stuck knives into him and punctured his lung . . . I'd put that first. And then thou shalt not go to bed without a man . . . then mental cruelty because it's far, far worse than anything physical. Physical injury, that's nothing compared with mental.

And what about—to covet?

Well, there's nothing wrong in wanting something; wishing you had it, is there? There's no harm in wishing. Then—honour thy father and mother—yes, that one—you must have respect.

Before your mates? . . .

Course yes . . . but our mum lives a long way away—no I don't write, not now—well how can I—tell her a load of lies about what I'm doing now. If I told her the truth it'd break her heart.

She, a pale prostitute of 19, married, two kids. And in an immaculately kept photo-album, with parents, her boy friends of long ago, her husband, their marriage (R.C.) and photos of the kiddies; one of the two babies and underneath in correct handwriting, slowly written: "God knows what I've done, and if you ever know you'll never forgive me, but I still love you and always will—the only good thing I've ever done. . . ."

He turned up on our doorstep, literally: worn out and without a job, starving, penniless, friendless. And for three months I fed him, as best I could and tried to find work for him, and lent him the money whenever he needed to go to Leicester and his old haunts. And for all that three months, he made no effort; too lazy to even go to the Labour Exchange and sign on the dole. He'd wake up, come along into the front room, curl on to the sofa with a blanket wrapped round him in front of a fire, and half-watch telly from three in the afternoon to the National Anthem. He wouldn't get up. I'd bring him a meal. Fetch him his cigarettes, even a glass of water or beer when we could afford it. If we were up in the morning and we went out for a meal, and we had a beer with it, he'd spill the beer across the tablecloth, or try being abusive to the waiter—deliberately. And when he stirred himself over to Leicester, cadging drinks all night he'd come back and, drunk, start on me—smash a bottle and try to slam it into my face; punch me around the room; threw me naked one night out of my own house, and he'd keep saying in drunken tears, "You're the only one who has ever been kind to me . . . you are the nearest I've ever had to a father or a brother—hit me, come on, put one on me, I'm no good—I'm dying, not physically, but inside myself—you wouldn't know but I'm killing myself—I'll never leave here till you throw me out". In the end, we starved him out, and he left, and I haven't seen him since. He is 19.

Another in the first strand: in and out of Borstal all his 22 years, he'd talk away: If he ever did vote, he'd vote Tory—no, there would never be prison reform. It was impossible—yes, property had to be respected. I mean, if I owned a house I'd kill anyone who tried anything on. And he'd go out in the cold and dark with his little bag, just like a plumber, only it was two in the morning. The hard men, the scrubbers. Satan's men, they'd like being called that. "Popular morality is now a waste-land littered with the debris of broken conventions". (Carstairs, Reith lecture.) They'd agree with that too, these iconoclasts.

If you, kind, critical readers will bear with me for a few lines I'd like to put forward a poetic idea: After Grandma Booker, before the present generation I think the key, the pioneer was the "builder"—the planner, the London School of Economics, the social construction man. He was the key, the ideal. It was to him that people stood up to ask for freedom and sex, and not—being given it—the many rebelled to become like those of the first strand, like Pinky in Graham Greene's *Brighton Rock*. They have a morality standard and it's the old one, but they don't believe it pays to practise it.

But for the new generation, the teenager, neither the old, nor the builder will fit as keys. Professor Carstairs' Reith lecture quote is meaningless. Mention morals and they don't know what morals are: not outright, like that. For they are out in a desert, a vacuum; a brave few searching and trying to build up a new freedom, a new moral code. They are outcasts, setting out for the promised land, which after all is what youth is mostly about, and were it not for Grandma Booker there would be no turning back.

Some pay only lip service to a search for magical anarchist freedom. Some, knowingly or half knowingly, try. The search is for something inside each person; for a new soul. The key for the raughter, the hard man, is Cain—partly because the presence of the Lord is rotten.

But for the other two strands of the three it is Ishmael: the bastard son, classless, looking for the oases in the desert that is so often only a mirage.

The beginners—those who live at home with their parents, under the old "dispensation".

. . . and you think about it—sex—and it frightens you and then you see it on the telly, all scientific or all mushy, like a fairy land with nothing you can recognize—and then you open the paper, and there's this lovely bit, from somewhere, all lying back half stripped with her belly button showing, and you think "God I'd like that" and then you think of Maureen—and Maureen—

. . . and you go out the house, and up the street to the herbalist, only you walk past the shop and then back again because you've got that queasy feeling, and you pluck up courage, and the bell goes dong-ding, and out he comes in his white coat and his nicotine stained yellow Charlie Chaplin moustache, and he says: "Yes?" You look at a spot a little above his head to say: "Three rubbers please" and you've done it, so you breathe again and stop sweating, and he says: "Three?; you can get four packets for 12 bob you know. That's saving a shilling you know. You want to club together with some of your mates—makes a saving you know," and it sounds great—sex, is it easy?—answer: yes, and at cut price too. They'll be giving Green Shield stamps away with them soon.

And you jump up and on the bus and you feel them hard in your inside breast pocket. And after the dance you go out, and your thighs start burning and you know the look in her eyes, and you know you've got the same look in yours—so you put your hand in your inside pocket, and they're still there—and you kiss her, and you sweat all over and you fondle her, and she makes back and you've a great whopper on, and your guts feel all gristle and all you can say is, like a dog, a whimper . . . "Help me, Maureen, help me love".

Well afterwards you curse yourself. It's not being a man is it?

They are like animals, locked in their cages most of the time, and then they're let out and they go wild and histrionic. You have to beware of them when you throw a party, because they haven't any sense of responsibility, or timing, or leisure. When they see a bed, they want to jump right in, only find out they can't do anything because they're all out of tune.

With those frustrations; with the wasted effort getting through the inhibitions. They can soon tire, and forget the precautions, or settle for the ease and security of marriage, often a marriage they're not really keen on. They are worn out by the sheer force of trying to live in a desert, and back they go to the old dispensation. . . . Back to Droitwich or Doncaster resolved to lead a suburban life; find a nice girl. To fight against the ghost of Grandma Booker on one's own is impossible, almost, and you either go all the way to become a raughter, or you sink back into a greyness and amorality.

The urban kibbutzim—here are the least unsuccessful of the Ishmaels, the ones who are feeling towards a new moral code. The twosome that set up home and don't get married and prove what Adam Faith said to the Archbishop, that "Teenage love can be a very delicate and beautiful thing and a harmless thing".

And the others who take a flat together and make it into a home, sharing their lives together. There is little wildness here. You can't when you've got a home to run. The tie of "family" doesn't mean blood but very often just the people you live with; and it can be stronger, at times, than that to one's blood family. Although it may seem immoral according to Moses, it's a search for a way of life, completely new, for a much more satisfactory moral code and this is something you can't even call morals because it is something one feels one's way into. But this life, I think, has more principles and more courage and more thought put into it than any grey passive permissiveness. For I think the greatest sin, is lack of application; a willingness to be fobbed off by the second rate—a sitting back and putting up with the no-morality, which is accepted, almost everywhere.

On the palais floor you have a steady, and she is it. You may have intercourse together. You may "respect" each other. She may be a virgin, or she may be not—but she certainly isn't a scrubber. Her reputation is white. If the boy wants it, there are always The Girls—the scrubbers; but he too must be careful: no girl wants a 102nd hand man. You don't steal, but if you can make something on the quiet then you do. Honour thy father and mother and raise children. You mind your own business, and covet everything that isn't yours. This brings me to the other, and socially more important personal moral, loyalty—or what made you pay for this copy of *New Society*, when you might have been able to nick one from the bookstand. This is a good question for all of us to ask ourselves.

Towards authority and public property any respect and loyalty, any fear there was (and there was never very much in working class communities) has gone. From the queer, the person who has been inside, the CNDer—from most of the young, authority has earned itself a scorn and contempt, and I think, justifiably.

I've got no respect for them, none at all. If I passed a shop and an old lady was getting beaten about, then I'd jump in and—no, even then I'd have second thoughts about helping the police . . . I'd never even ask one of them for the time . . . I've got my pride, and it's got to go lower than this before I take National Assistance. . . . If I passed a shop, and it was a straight burglary, with no violence and no one getting hurt, then I'd pass by. Good luck to them.

Towards the neighbourhood, the corner shop, the people next door —here there has been a decline, and it's one that I myself regret. It took me a whole evening to stop our nearest pawn shop from being rifled. People who borrow a saucepan from next door, take their time returning it. When next door was robbed of a fiver at Christmas I bought her a bottle of whisky. Everyone thought I was mad. But in living in an urban kibbutz, these can be reversed, for often you have to use the corner shop, to cash the postal orders, cheques, to obtain food on the slate. The personal touches, no matter how much you use the Supermarkets, are too valuable to lose. We mustn't lose them.

Loyalty to friends is now at times above the family—for in living together you found new families of your own, that have nothing to do with blood. Gran will say "blood tells" but not so much. Important is loyalty to the way of life you have made for yourself since leaving home, or school, or growing up—to your mates, who can come from other families, other areas.

Loyalty to the family is now confined to mother, father and one or two special brothers or sisters: only to the closest, the next of kin, and those relations who have become friends.

But why don't you steal? What stops you? "You don't get away with silly things like that", but the fear of authority has lessened. Now it's rather: "I wouldn't sell myself, my pride, my self-respect—not for a handful of silver, or nothing".

Never enjoy wearing stuff you'd pinch because someone pinched my sweater once and it hurts. I value my self-respect more than Woolworths.

It's back to Grandma Booker. The important thing is yourself, and your pride. The greatest sin is suicide, despair. You must believe in yourself, have a loyalty to your word, and to your self-respect. You don't rob yourself of that, and you don't rob your own, your mates either. The ones who are most likely to go in for the little thievings are not the criminal, or the ones in their flats and cellars, but the ones who still live at home, for whom going out is a raid, of licence in everything.

And the first commandment, and the most frequently broken must be: thou shalt not kill thyself. In the long run, the emphasis has shifted from the Old to the New Testament. We must love one another. From the negative to the positive. This is the only base that will work. The Moses morality is in the melting pot, but the fumes of Grandma Booker are all around. Less scared of the world and God than she was, the young are willing to stand up and ask, demand life. The important thing is the way you live, and not technicalities of virginity and birth control. The importance is of keeping a magic in life, not of a one day, some dream future, but The Now.

If I have any fear, it is not that this generation is more promiscuous, but that they are giving up too easily, through lack of guts, support and staying power, their movings towards freedom, happiness and love. Morally, we're all in the same melting pot. Judgment mustn't be in a question of degree. We're not fit to judge, any of us. We have got to get together, in all ways. If not, then we are lost.

6

Struggling Through the Doldrums

D W WINNICOTT

25 APRIL 1963

The present world-wide interest in adolescence and in the problems of the adolescent indicates the special conditions of the times we live in. If we wish to explore this area of psychology we may as well first ask ourselves, do adolescent boys and girls wish to be understood? The answer, I think, is no. In fact adults should hide among themselves what they come to understand of adolescence. It would be absurd to write a book for adolescents on the subject of adolescence, because this period of life is one which must be lived. It is essentially a time of personal discovery. Each individual is engaged in a living experience, a problem of existing, and of the establishment of an identity.

In fact there exists only one real cure for adolescence: maturation. This and the passage of time do, in the end, result in the emergence of the adult person. The process cannot be hurried up, though indeed it can be broken into and destroyed by clumsy handling; or it can wither up from within when there is psychiatric illness in the individual. We do sometimes need to be reminded that although adolescence is something we always have with us, each adolescent boy or girl grows up in the course of a few years into an adult. Irritation with the phenomena of adolescence can easily be evoked by careless reference to adolescence as a permanent problem, forgetting that each individual is in the process of becoming a responsible society minded adult.

If we examine the maturational processes we see that the boy or girl in this age phase is having to deal with important changes associated with puberty. A boy or girl develops sexual capacity and secondary sexual manifestations appear. The way in which the individual copes with these changes and deals with the anxieties arising out of them is based, to quite a large extent, on the pattern organized in early childhood when there was a similar phase of rapid emotional and physical growth. In this earlier phase those who were well cared for and who were healthy did develop what is called the Oedipus complex, that is to say, the capacity to be able to deal with triangular relationships—to accept the full force of the capacity to love and the complications that result.

The healthy child comes to adolescence already equipped with a personal method for dealing with new feelings, for tolerating distress, and for warding off situations which involve intolerable anxiety. Also derived from the experiences of each adolescent's early infancy and childhood are certain inherited and acquired personal characteristics and tendencies, residual illness patterns associated with failure rather than success in the management of feelings that belong to infancy and the toddler age. Patterns which have been formed in relation to infantile and early childhood experiences necessarily include a great deal that is unconscious and there is also much that the child does not know because it has not yet been experienced.

Always the question arises, how shall this personality organization meet the new instinctual capacity? How will the pubertal changes be accommodated in the personality pattern that is specific to the boy or girl in question? Moreover, how shall each one deal with something that really is new: the power to destroy and even to kill, a power which did not complicate the feelings of hatred that were experienced at the toddler age?

The part played by the environment is immensely significant at this stage, so much so that in a descriptive account it is best to assume the continued existence and interest of the child's own father and mother and the wider family organization. A great deal of the work of a psychiatrist concerns the troubles that arise relative to environmental failure at some stage or other, and this fact only emphasizes the vital importance of the environment and of the family setting. In the case of the vast majority of adolescents the environment can be assumed to be good enough. Most adolescents do in fact achieve adult maturity, even if in the process they give their parents headaches. But even in the best circumstances where the environment facilitates the maturational processes the individual adolescent still has many personal problems and many difficult phases to negotiate.

THE ISOLATION OF THE INDIVIDUAL

The adolescent is essentially an isolate. It is from a position of isolation that he or she launches out into what may result in relationships. It is the individual relationships, one by one, that eventually lead to socialization. The adolescent is repeating an essential phase of infancy, for the infant too is an isolate, at least until he or she has been able to establish the capacity for relating to objects that are outside magical control. The infant becomes able to recognize and to welcome the existence of objects that are not part of the infant, but this is an achievement. The adolescent repeats this struggle.

It is as if the adolescent must start from a state of isolation. Relationships must first be tried out on subjective objects. In this way we sometimes see young adolescents as collections of isolates, attempting at the same time to form an aggregate through the adoption of mutual ideas, ideals, and ways of dressing and living. It is as if they can become grouped on account of their mutual interests and concerns. They can of course achieve a group if they are attacked as a group, but this is a grouping that is reactive, and after the end of the persecution the grouping ceases. It is therefore not satisfactory because it has no dynamic from within.

The sexual experiences of the younger adolescents are coloured by this phenomenon of isolation, and by the need that exists for association on the basis of mutual interest. Also is it not true that the boy or girl at this stage does not yet know whether he or she will be homosexual, heterosexual, or just narcissistic? It can indeed be painful for a young adolescent to realize that he only loves himself, and this can be worse for a boy than for a girl because society tolerates narcissistic elements in a girl but is impatient of self-love in a boy. Often there is a long period of uncertainty in the boy or girl as to whether a sex urge will turn up at all.

Urgent masturbatory activity may be at this stage a repeated getting rid of sex rather than a form of sex experience. That is to say, it may be a repeated attempt to deal with a purely physiological problem which becomes urgent before the full meaning of sex dawns. Indeed, compulsive heterosexual or homosexual activities may also serve the purpose of getting rid of sex tension at a time when there has not yet developed a capacity for union between whole human beings. Union between whole human beings is more likely to appear first in aim inhibited sex play or in affectionate behaviour with the accent on dependence or interdependence. Here again is a personal pattern waiting to join up with the new instinctual developments, but in the long meanwhile adolescents have to find relief from sex tension, so that compulsive masturbation is to be expected, and it may bother the young adolescent because of its senselessness.

It is not even necessarily pleasurable, and it produces its own complications. The investigator, of course, seldom gets to know the truth about these matters, which are very secret, and indeed a good motto for the investigator would be: whoever asks questions must expect to be told lies.

THE TIME FOR ADOLESCENCE

Is it not a sign of the health of society that teenagers are able to be adolescent at the right time, that is to say at the age that covers pubertal growth? Among primitive peoples the pubertal changes are either hidden under taboos or else the adolescent is turned into an adult in the space of a few weeks or months by certain rites and ordeals. At present in our society adults are being formed by natural processes out of adolescents who move forward because of growth tendencies. This may easily mean that the new adults of today have strength and stability and maturity.

Naturally, there must be a price to pay in toleration and patience; and also this development puts a new strain on society, for it is distressing for adults who have been themselves defrauded of adolescence to watch the boys and girls all round them in a state of florid adolescence.

For me there are three main social developments that, together, have altered the whole climate for adolescents:

Venereal Disease No Deterrent

Venereal disease is no longer a bogy. The spirochaete and the gonococcus are no longer (as they certainly were felt to be 50 years ago) agents of a punishing God. Now they can be dealt with by penicillin and by appropriate antibiotics. I remember very clearly a girl somewhere after the First World War. She told me that it was only the fear of venereal disease that had kept her from being a prostitute. She was horrified at the idea I put forward in a simple conversation that venereal disease might one day be preventable or curable. She said she could not imagine how she could have got through her adolescence (and she was only just coming through it) without this fear which she had used in order to keep straight. She is now the mother of a large family and you would call her a normal sort of person; but she had yet to engage in her adolescent struggle and the challenge of her own instincts. She had a difficult time. She did a bit of thieving, and lying, but she emerged an adult.

Contraception

The development of contraceptive techniques has given the adolescent the freedom to explore. This freedom is new, the freedom to find out about sexuality and sensuality when there is not only an absence of a wish for parenthood, but also a wish to avoid bringing into the world an unwanted and unparented baby. Of course, accidents happen and will happen, and these accidents lead to unfortunate and dangerous abortions or to the birth of illegitimate children.

But in examining the problem of adolescence we must accept the fact, I suggest, that the modern adolescent can explore, if he or she has a mind to, the whole area of sensuous living, without suffering the mental agony that accidental conception involves. This is only partly true because the mental agony associated with the fear of an accident remains, but the problem has been altered in the course of the last 30 years by this new factor. The mental agony, we can now see, comes not so much from fear as from the individual child's guilt sense. I do not mean that every child has an inborn guilt sense, but I mean that in health the child develops in a very complicated way a sense of right and wrong and a capacity for experiencing a sense of guilt; and each child has ideals, and has an idea of what he or she wants for the future.

Very strong conscious and unconscious factors are involved, conflicting feelings and fears that can only be explained in terms of the individual's total fantasy. For instance, one girl felt compelled to plant two illegitimate children on her mother before settling down to have her own family in marriage. The motivation included revenge related to the girl's place in her own family, and it also included the idea that she owed her mother two babies and that she must discharge this debt before getting on with establishing her own life. There can be extremely complex motivations for behaviour at this age—and indeed at all ages—and any simplification violates the truth. It is fortunate that in most cases of adolescent difficulty the family attitude (which is in itself complex) restrains wild acting out and takes the boy or girl past awkward episodes.

An End of Fighting

The hydrogen bomb is perhaps producing more profound changes even than the first two of the characteristics of our age that I have listed here. The atom bomb affects the relationship between adult society and the adolescent tide which seems to be for ever coming in. It is not so much that this new bomb symbolizes a maniacal episode, a moment of infantile incontinence expressed in terms of fantasy that has become true—rage that has turned into actual destruction. Gunpowder already symbolized all this and the deeper aspects of madness, and the world was long ago altered by the invention of gunpowder which gave reality to magic. The more general result of the threat of nuclear war is that in effect it means that *there is not going to be another war*. It can be argued that there might be a war any minute in some place or other in the world, but because of the new bomb we know we can no longer solve a social problem by organizing for a new war. Nothing exists any longer therefore that can justify our providing strong military or naval discipline. We cannot supply this for our young men and we cannot justify supplying it for our children unless we call on something in ourselves which must be called cruelty or revenge.

If it makes no sense any longer to deal with our difficult adolescents by preparing them to fight for their king and country, we have lost something that we have been in the habit of using, and so we are thrown back on this problem, that there is adolescence, a thing in itself, with which society must learn to live.

Adolescence could be said to be a state of prepotency. In the imaginative life of man potency is not just a matter of the active and passive of intercourse; it includes the idea of man's victory over man, and the girl's admiration of the victor. All this, I am suggesting, now has to be wrapped up in the mystique of the coffee bar and in the occasional disturbance with knives. Adolescence now has to contain itself, to contain itself in a way it has never had to do before, and we have to reckon that adolescence has pretty violent potential.

When we think of the occasional atrocities of modern youth we must weigh them against the deaths that belong to the war that is no more to take place, and against all the cruelty that belongs to the war that is not going to be, and against all the free sexuality which belongs to every war that has ever been but is not going to be again. So adolescence has come to stay, and along with it the violence and sex that is inherent in it.

These three changes that I have listed are among those that are having an effect on our social concern, and one of the first lessons that we have to learn is that adolescence is not something that can be hustled off the stage by false manoeuvres.

THE STRUGGLE TO FEEL REAL

Is it not a prime characteristic of adolescents that they do not accept false solutions? They have a fierce morality which accepts only that which feels real, and this is a morality that also characterizes infancy. It is a morality that goes much deeper than wickedness, and has as its motto, "to thine own self be true". The adolescent is engaged in trying to find the self to be true to.

This is linked with the fact that, as I have said, the cure for adolescence is the passage of time, a fact which has very little meaning for the adolescent who rejects one cure after another on account of some false element in it. Once he can admit that compromise is allowable, he may discover various ways in which the relentlessness of essential truth can be softened. For instance, there is the solution by identification with parent figures, and there can be a premature maturity in terms of sex, and there can be a shift of emphasis from violence to physical prowess in athletics or from the bodily functions to intellectual attainment or achievement. In general, adolescents reject these helps, because they have not yet become able to accept compromise; instead they have to go through what might be called a doldrums area, a phase in which they feel futile.

I think of a boy who lives with his mother in a small flat. He is very intelligent, but he wastes his grammar school opportunities. He lies in bed threatening to take an overdose of something, and playing lugubrious jazz on the record player. He sometimes locks his mother out, and she has to get the police to help her into her own flat. He has many friends, and suddenly the flat comes to life when they all come round and bring their own beer and food; the party may go on all night or a whole week-end. There is a good deal of sex and the boy himself has a firm girl friend, and his suicidal impulses are related to ideas of her being indifferent to him.

He lacks a father figure, but he does not really know this. He does not know what he wants to be, and this increases his sense of futility. Opportunities come his way but he neglects them. He cannot leave his mother although she and he are tired of each other.

An adolescent who entirely avoids compromise, especially the use of identifications and vicarious experience, must start from scratch, ignoring all that has been worked out in the past history of our culture. Adolescents can be seen struggling to start again as if they had nothing they could take over from anyone. They can be seen to be forming groups on the basis of minor uniformities, and on the basis of some sort of group appearance which belongs to locality and to age. They can be seen searching for a form of identification which does not let them down in their struggle, the struggle for identity, the struggle to feel real, the struggle not to fit into an adult-assigned role, but to go through whatever has to be gone through. They feel unreal except in so far as they are refusing the false solutions, and feeling unreal leads them to do certain things which are only too real from the point of view of society. Society does in fact get very much caught up with this curious thing about adolescents: the mixture of defiance and dependence which characterizes them. Those who look after adolescents will find themselves puzzled how it can be that a boy or girl can be defiant to a degree and at the same time so dependent as to be childish, even infantile. Moreover parents find themselves paying out money to enable children to be defiant, although of course it is the parents who suffer from the defiance. This is a good example of the way in which those who theorize and write and talk are operating in a layer that is different from the one in which adolescents live. Parents or parent substitutes are faced with urgent problems of management. They are not concerned with theory but with the impact of the one on the other, the adolescent and the parent.

So it is possible to gather together a list of what we may think are some of the needs of adolescents:

The need to avoid the false solution: the need to feel real or to tolerate not feeling at all;

The need to defy—in a setting in which their dependence is met and can be relied on to be met;

The need repeatedly to prod society so that society's antagonism is manifest, and can be met with antagonism.

HEALTH AND ILLNESS

That which shows in the normal adolescent is related to that which shows in various kinds of ill persons. For instance, the idea of the repudiation of the false solution corresponds with the schizophrenic patient's inability to compromise; and in contrast with this there is psychoneurotic ambivalence and also the deceptiveness and self-deception to be found in healthy people. Again, the need to feel real corresponds with the feelings of unreality associated with psychotic depression, with depersonalization. And the need to defy corresponds with one aspect of the antisocial tendency as it appears in delinquency.

From this it follows that in a group of adolescents the various tendencies tend to be represented by the more ill members of the group. One member of a group takes an overdose of a drug, another lies in bed in a depression, another is free with the flick knife. In each case there are grouped a band of adolescent isolates behind the ill individual whose extreme symptom has impinged on society. Yet in the majority of these individuals, whether or not they get involved, there was not enough drive behind the tendency to bring the symptom into inconvenient existence and to produce a social reaction. The ill one had to act for the others.

To repeat: if the adolescent is to get through this developmental stage by natural process, then there must be expected a phenomenon which could be called adolescent doldrums. Society needs to include this as a permanent feature and to tolerate it, to go to meet it, but not to cure it. The question is, has our society the health to do this?

Complicating this issue is the fact that some individuals are too ill (either with psychoneurosis or with depression or with schizophrenia) to reach a stage of emotional development that could be called adolescence, or they can only reach this in a highly distorted way. It has not been possible to include in this brief statement a picture of severe psychiatric illness as it appears at this age level. Nevertheless there is

6—YINS

one type of illness that cannot be set aside in any statement about adolescence: delinquency.

Here again, there is a close relationship between the normal difficulties of adolescence and the abnormality that may be called the antisocial tendency. The difference between these two states does not lie so much in the clinical picture each presents as in the dynamics—in the origin— of each. At the root of the antisocial tendency there is always a deprivation. It may simply be that the mother, at a critical time, was in a withdrawn state or depressed, or it may be that the family broke up. Even a minor deprivation occurring at a difficult moment in the life of a child may have a lasting result by overstraining the available defences. Behind the antisocial tendency there is always a history of some health and then an interruption, after which things were never the same again. The antisocial child is searching in some way or other, violently or gently, to get the world to acknowledge its debt, trying to make the world reform the framework which got broken up. In the root of the antisocial tendency is deprivation.

In the root of healthy adolescence in general it is not possible to say that there is inherently a deprivation, but still there is something in a diffused way which is the same but in a degree just not strong enough to overstrain the available defences. This means that in the group that the adolescent finds to identify with, the extreme members of the group are acting for the total group. All sorts of things in the adolescent's struggle, the stealing, the knives, the breaking out and the breaking in; all these have to be contained in the dynamic of this group sitting round listening to blue jazz, or whatever is on.

If nothing happens, the individual members begin to feel unsure of the reality of their protest, and yet they are not in themselves disturbed enough to do an antisocial act. But if in the group there is an antisocial boy or girl who is willing to do the antisocial thing which produces a social reaction, this makes all the others cohere, makes them feel real, and temporarily gives the group a structure. Each will be loyal and will support the individual who will act for the group, although not one of them would have approved of the thing that the extreme antisocial did.

I think that this principle applies to the use of other kinds of illness. The suicide attempt of one of the members is very important to all the others. Or, one of them cannot get up, he is paralyzed with depression. The others all know this is happening. Such happenings belong to the whole group and the group is shifting and the individuals are changing their groups, but somehow the individual members of the group use the extremes to help themselves to feel real, in their struggle to endure this doldrums period.

It comes down to a problem of: how to be adolescent during adolescence? This is an extremely brave thing for anybody to be. It does not mean that we grown-ups have to be saying: "Look at these dear little adolescents having their adolescence; we must put up with everything and let our windows get broken". This is not the point. The point is that we are challenged and we meet the challenge as part of the function of adult living. But we meet the challenge rather than set out to cure what is essentially healthy.

The big threat from the adolescent is the threat to the bit of ourselves that has not really had its adolescence. This bit of ourselves makes us resent these people being able to have their phase of the doldrums and makes us want to find a solution for them. There are hundreds of false solutions. Anything we say or do is wrong. We give support and we are wrong, we withdraw support and that is wrong too. We dare not be "understanding". But in the course of time we find that this adolescent boy and this adolescent girl has come out of the doldrums phase and is now able to begin identifying with society, with parents, and with wider groups, and to do so without feeling threatened with personal extinction.

7

What To Do About Pep Pills

P H CONNELL

20 FEBRUARY 1964

There have been many reports recently, in the popular press, of drug taking by teenagers. Headlines such as "16 year old boy started taking purple hearts" (and later began to steal). " 'Beware, the pep pill addict' doctors told"; " 'Purple hearts' to change shape and colour?"; "Parents urge war on 'pep pill barons' "; "Poisons Board Drive to outlaw 'pep' pill traffickers"; "Purple Hearts: the 'mystique' factor", etc., are now commonplace and indicate the presence of a problem which needs to be examined. Are these reports exaggerations of the present situation? Is there really a problem? What drugs are being used? Are any steps needed to deal with the situation? What does it all add up to?

The amphetamines—the group of drugs commonly used for pep effects—include such drugs as amphetamine itself (Benzedrine), dexamphetamine (Dexedrine), methylamphetamine (Methedrine) and phenmetrazine (Preludin). These drugs can be combined with bar- biturates as has been done in the case of Drinamyl (the purple heart tablets which are really blue but shaped like a heart), Anxine, Desbutal, etc. The reason for the combination with barbiturates—drugs which help to calm the nervous system and promote sleep—was to counteract one of the undesirable effects of the amphetamines, namely the effect of keeping the patient awake and causing restlessness (hence the term "wake-amine" which has been used by the popular press).

The amphetamines were developed originally in the late 1920s to offer an alternative to ephedrine in the treatment of such conditions as asthma, since at that time ephedrine—a substance obtained from the Chinese herb ma-huang—was in short supply. The stimulating effect of amphetamine on the central nervous system was soon discovered and possible therapeutic uses suggested.

The main effects of therapeutic doses of amphetamine can be tabulated as follows, and are due to stimulation of the sympathetic nervous system leading to:

euphoria (an exaggerated sense of well-being),
lessening of feelings of fatigue,
production of wakefulness,
suppression of appetite,
tendency to raise the blood pressure,
tendency to loquaciousness,
dryness of the mouth,
palpitations,
irritability,
headache,
impotence,
inability to relax.

The latter six reactions which may occur with therapeutic dosage in some patients are clearly undesirable side effects.

The amphetamines have been used in a number of medical disorders including congestion of the mucous membranes of the upper respiratory tract (inhalers), epilepsy, barbiturate poisoning, alcoholism, psychopathic state, behaviour disorders in children, enuresis, depression, obesity and narcolepsy (a condition in which the individual may go to sleep suddenly, often during the day, perhaps while at work). Today, however, the indications for the use of the amphetamines in medical practice are greatly diminished and there are some authorities who consider there is no place for them. It is certainly true to state that these drugs are only rarely used, nowadays, in psychiatric practice, though recent studies in Liverpool and in Newcastle-upon-Tyne have shown that they may be widely used by family doctors, and that prescriptions for these drugs comprise a large proportion of the total National Health Service drug bill.

The fact that abuse of amphetamine took place was only slowly realized and it was not until individuals were found who showed severe mental disturbance, or who had forged prescriptions and were taking large doses of the drug, that action was taken to control the sale of these drugs. It was the discovery that persons bought amphetamine inhalers (which contained the equivalent of about 110 five mgm tablets of amphetamine) and ingested the contents that led to action being taken in 1957, and to the drugs being confined to Schedule IV of the Poisons Rules, meaning that they could only be supplied on medical prescription. It is still not an offence to be in possession of these drugs.

Habituates and addicts may take large numbers of tablets of the amphetamine group of drugs: 30 Drinamyl tablets at a time is not uncommon. Some of the toxic effects of misuse of these drugs are:

> inability to sleep,
> restlessness,
> excessively dry mouth,
> dilated pupils,
> excessive talkativeness,
> gross euphoria,
> overactivity (leading perhaps, to car accidents, aggressive
>   behaviour, etc.),
> trembling,
> unsteadiness of gait,
> gross lack of inhibition in behaviour,
> a severe mental disturbance in which delusions and hallucinations

may occur—particularly of a kind in which the individual feels that everyone is against him, there are gangs or police chasing him and wanting to harm him, and with hallucinations of animals, police cars, crowds, etc., which are not, in fact, there at all. This is what the pill taker calls "the horrors". During this mental disturbance the individual can be dangerous.

It is not surprising that these powerful drugs, with their ability to provide an artificially produced sense of well-being, have been the cause of illegal actions. In Japan, immediately after the war, a large illegal industry manufacturing methylamphetamine (Metherdine, Pervitin) grew up and teenagers in Japan were even giving themselves hypodermic injections into their own veins (called main-lining). A number of murders were attributed to the effects of this drug which was eventually brought under stricter supervision. The problem of amphetamine taking has also been widespread in the United States.

WHERE DRUGS COME FROM

Recently, the Ministry of Health has appealed to all family doctors in the National Health Service to be more careful in prescribing amphetamine tablets and barbiturates and to keep their official prescription pads in a safe place. But these drugs may be being illegally manufactured in this country.

The other drug, which is said to be becoming popular with teenagers is marihuana. This drug is not prescribed therapeutically by doctors.

Obtained from the plant *Cannabis Indica* or Sativa (hemp, hashish), marihuana has been used as a euphoriant in the Middle East for over 500 years. It can be eaten, drunk or smoked. It is usually used in the form of cigarettes (reefers) since the action of the drug then comes on almost immediately after inhalation. The plant grows wild in the United States.

The effects of euphoria, a sense of floating in the air, lightness, volubility, increased physical activity, sometimes with suspicion, leading into a state described as a "delicious and confused lassitude in which distance and time intervals appear subjectively elastic".

Intoxication leads to a state of hilarious elation, with disinhibition, distortion in time and space perception, appetite increased (craving for sweets is common), characteristic odour to the breath, reddening of the conjunctivae of the eye, dilation of the pupil, dry mouth and parched throat, involuntary twitching, disturbed gait and loss of balance, and sometimes a severe mental state in which there is confusion, disturbance of the stream of thought, disturbance of memory illusions and hallucinations.

In the case of the amphetamines and also marihuana, the state of recovery from the intoxication is often one of feeling "down", low spirited, lacking in energy and with a strong desire to take more.

The fact of teenagers and others taking the drugs such as amphetamine, amphetamine plus barbiturate and marihuana, is not, in my submission, under dispute. I myself recently saw a boy of 15 years who had been the round of the Soho and other clubs in London and described taking purple hearts, dexamphetamine, amphetamine and other drugs, including what might have been by his description librium (a tranquillizer), amyl nitrite (which is in a capsule and is sniffed) and cigarettes containing marihuana. He had had an episode of paranoid psychosis (the horrors) and was having great difficulty in refraining from going back to the clubs and obtaining more supplies. He said that the purple hearts were 6d. or sometimes 9d. each, amyl nitrite capsules were 5s. each, and Benzedrine and Dexedrine tablets were 6d. each. He had taken 50 Drinamyl tablets (purple hearts) during one hour preceding the attack of the horrors which came on an hour or two later.

The large majority of well-adjusted individuals will either not wish to take these drugs or will try them for fun, and will not become addicted. However, an unstable person, one who is emotionally immature, as so many of our teenagers today seem to be, will be more likely to become habituated or addicted to these drugs and, moreover, such individuals will be more likely to seek out the "kicks" because of their basic personality weaknesses—a passing phase in many teenagers. There is, therefore, potential harm in these drugs, though the extent of the harm and the number of individuals involved is not known officially, since so few either get to the psychiatrist or to the direct notice of the police or officials of the Courts.

It is my view that the problem of drug taking, particularly among teenagers, is more widespread than official reports would indicate and should be taken seriously. Dependency and habituation certainly occur in a proportion of individuals who may undertake criminal acts to obtain the drug or to obtain money in order to obtain the drug. Its extent is unknown.

The possibility of individuals taking these drugs being introduced to even more dangerous drugs certainly exists. The clubs concerned are sometimes frequented by homosexuals, prostitutes, and individuals addicted to morphia, heroin, etc., and the possibility of contamination is definitely present. The extent of this possible contamination is not known, since addicts to morphine, heroin, etc., are very much more careful about their activities, or at least the suppliers of the drugs are more careful because of the legal aspects and penalties if caught. The official opinion is that there are less than 500 narcotic addicts known to the authorities. Some evidence is coming to light that this figure may be an underestimate and that introduction of teenagers and young adults to morphine and heroin may be taking place.

How can the problem be tackled? So far as teenagers are concerned, it is likely that the majority are, in fact, going through an unsettled adolescence, partly because of the tendency in our modern culture to avoid the more positive aspects of child rearing and for parental supervision and control during adolescence to be absent or very diluted. It would seem reasonable that steps should be taken to control these drugs more stringently in order that opportunities for drug taking are minimized. This could be done in two main ways. Firstly, by making it an offence to be in possession of the drugs, and, secondly, by placing those drugs which are prescribed by doctors for therapeutic purposes on the same control list as are morphine, heroin, etc. These would not completely remove the evil but, as preventive measures could be most valuable. In this way the emotionally immature teenager would have some measure of protection.

SIGNS OF INSTABILITY

The other method of approach is to look at those persons who do become habituated or addicted to the pep drugs and evaluate the kind of personality problems from which they suffer. These problems are likely to be associated with and caused by a combination of many factors, including genetic, child-rearing practices, family disturbances, marital disharmony, educational difficulties, social and cultural stresses of our time and including within their scope the whole complex of the relationship between the individual, his family, and society.

This means two main avenues of approach. Firstly, research into the causes of the personality difficulties and in this instance full enquiry and examination of those individuals who show problems of habituation to these drugs. In London, it would be feasible for referral of such cases to be made to one hospital in order that there can be a concentration of effort by a team of workers in the one hospital, rather than the occasional case being seen at a large number of hospitals. This leads to many doctors, social workers, and so on, having very limited experience of the problem and to the absence of any real experts in this field. As it is now, advice is given to the Government and its committees by individuals who have little experience in the field concerning which they are advising.

The second avenue of approach is a general one. It is concerned with the long term and difficult question of how to help our society, by all possible means, to produce children who have a better chance to grow

8
Moral Education in Chaos
JAMES HEMMING

5 SEPTEMBER 1963

In a stable moral system, dominant ideas, values, and the rituals by which they are sustained in social consciousness, blend into a complex whole which is self-perpetuating. Inevitably social convenience penetrates and influences the moral system, leading to conflicts and inconsistencies, as when Christianity has tolerated the slave trade or the hanging of small boys, but the whole system holds together reasonably well so long as the dominant ideas remain inviolate in the minds of the community as a whole. The traditional dominant ideas of our moral system stem from orthodox Christian teaching about what man is, how he is to be valued, and where he fits into the scheme of creation. Moral education is in a state of confusion in British schools today because many of the traditional Christian ideas of our culture are no longer dominant in the minds of the community, but the schools are expected to behave as if they were.

The grip of the idea system of orthodox Christianity upon our minds has not been weakened by some organized attack upon it but by the course of events. Our knowledge of man and his development has gradually accumulated to the point when, for most people, ideas that were the backbone of religious orthodoxy not long ago are now quite unacceptable. To quote Sir Julian Huxley: "Man was not created in his present form a few thousand years ago. Mankind is not descended from a single couple. Children are not born with a load of original sin derived from a 'Fall' ." (*Nature*, 5 January 1963.) Man, in fact, is not a renegade angel but a rising animal and, in terms of the biological time scale, not a hoary failure but a struggling beginner.

The new cosmology also militates against the ready acceptance of the traditional idea system. Its one-world emphasis makes it less and less appropriate for explaining the position and destiny of man in a universe in which other conscious life almost certainly exists. Modern psychology, with its new approaches to motivation and guilt, conflicts at certain points too. The gap between what orthodoxy demands and what is intellectually tenable to an informed modern mind has been growing over the years and has now reached such proportions that leading churchmen, normally identified with the traditional idea system, are forced into a degree of revolt against orthodox Christian theology that is, in some cases, almost total—witness Dr J. A. T. Robinson's *Honest to God* and the essays of Dr A. R. Vidler and his Cambridge colleagues published under the title of *Soundings*. That these writings should come within the same period of time as the campaigns of a fundamentalist like Dr Billy Graham illustrates the confusion of the traditional idea system. Its rejection in the face of hopeful expectations for its revival is not to be assessed as a measure of national wickedness but rather as proof that the new knowledge about man, gradually permeating the mass of the community, precludes the acceptance of orthodoxy.

Yet, by an accident of history, Christian orthodoxy is built into the school curriculum as the official foundation for moral education. This arose from the special circumstances of the 1944 Education Act. At this time not only were people concerned to foster moral education, but the future of the denominational schools also created a problem. These schools needed state help but wished to remain as much as possible under their own control. But public finance made inevitable a degree of public control however distasteful this might be to the denominations. In the end a compromise was worked out which included, by way of compensation to the churches, the assurance that all schools should include in their curricula a daily act of worship and regular religious instruction. To quote the Act:

> Subject to the provisions of this section, the school day in every county school and in every voluntary school shall begin with collective worship, on the part of all pupils in attendance at the school, and the arrangements made therefore shall provide for a single act of

worship attended by all such pupils unless, in the opinion of the local education authority or, in the case of a voluntary school, of the managers or governors thereof, the school premises are such as to make it impracticable to assemble them for that purpose.

Subject to the provisions of this section, religious instruction shall be given in every county school and in every voluntary school.

(Education Act, 1944, Section 25, paragraphs 1 and 2.)

The content of the compulsory R.I. course was left unspecified in detail. The local education authorities were given the obligation of providing for their areas "agreed syllabuses" which were to be free from denominational bias. These syllabuses were drafted by committees representing the local education committees, the local churches and representatives of the teaching profession. The syllabuses varied considerably in content. All were prepared with great care, and some have provided leads from Bible instruction into practical life through the study of the lives of great Christians. Some syllabuses have recently been revised, for example that of the Bristol Education Committee. But all have the common feature that they teach Christian orthodoxy. Critical and comparative approaches, when included, are postponed until late in the secondary school course. Hence the curious fact that the only subject of instruction which is officially compulsory in the curriculum of the schools of England and Wales is religious instruction. The effect has been to put the onus of moral education on to the daily act of worship, and religious instruction as laid down in the Act. All the agreed syllabuses are offered not as mandates but as guides, but they nevertheless represent the official basis for moral education in the schools of England and Wales. They have thus given the stamp of authority to a traditional system which has been breaking down socially and, indeed, globally.

This confusion has increased as another schism develops within the content of Christian teaching itself. The two great architects of Christian thought, Jesus and St Paul, disagree on a number of fundamental issues. "O wretched man that I am! Who shall deliver me from the body of this death?" is a very different statement from "The Kingdom of God is within you". Jesus was life-affirming; Paul was life-weary. Jesus believed in man; Paul did not. Jesus liked and respected women; Paul regarded them as inferior human beings. Jesus was tolerant of all misdemeanours except hypocrisy and self-righteousness; Paul was intolerant and punitive. The prudishness that was an impediment and a disgrace to Christianity for hundreds of years, and still lives on in society, derived from St Paul, not from Jesus.

Pauline ideas about man and his destiny are at a discount today. Modern youth, growing up among people who sunbathe almost naked without a vestige of shame or guilt, who regard the body as a valid source of intense pleasure, who evaluate sexual frigidity as a human incompleteness and not a human virtue, is unlikely to respond sympathetically to all that element of Christian orthodoxy which is sin-soaked and life-rejecting.

The compulsion of the schools to run with the hare and hunt with the hounds in a high-pressure commercial society further complicates the moral climate surrounding our young people as they grow. The schools like to feel above the rat-race, concerned with altruistic rather than utilitarian ideas. But social pressure drives them inexorably back to the values imposed by an acquisitive, individualistic society. Officially they sustain the non-acquisitive values of Christianity; unofficially they are dedicated to the hunt for status and possessions. So children whose university prospects are weighed at the time they leave infant school—as starters or non-starters in the examination obstacle race—are advised in R.I. to "take no thought for the morrow". The Sermon on the Mount instructs them "Judge not, that ye be not judged", but the paraphernalia of judgment surrounds them at every point. Children who in their own lives find little tolerance of repeated misdemeanours somehow have to couple this with the edict of Jesus that you should forgive an erring brother not just seven times but "until seventy times seven". The acquisition of good jobs is used as a spur to effort along with the R.I. teaching that riches do not lead to happiness. Children study the commandments and read that it is against the will of God to make the likeness "of anything that is in heaven above, or in the earth beneath, or in the water under the earth" and are then busily put to work painting, carving, and doing pottery. Such inconsistency could pass without notice in earlier times; today it serves to mark off R.I. as something incomprehensible and inapplicable to everyday life. The position is, of course, that some of the dominant ideas of orthodox Christianity can transfer into a scientific age and some cannot, while some, though highly applicable to modern life, are inconveniently critical of acquisitive individualism.

The effect of this intolerable confusion is to bring into disrepute the very machinery built into the schools by the 1944 Act with a view to safeguarding moral education. A recent inquiry into the religious beliefs of sixth form boys carried out by D. S. Wright in Leicester produced the following percentages:

Always take morning assembly seriously	23
Sometimes take morning assembly seriously	43
Never take morning assembly seriously	34

Questions about R.I. elicited an unenthusiastic response. And this at a time when young people are showing a lively interest in moral and religious issues. Other inquiries support the weak impact of R.I. More than half the 120 schools reported on in *Religion In Schools*, the Unitarian and Free Church study, in 1962, gave the assessment that R.I. "excited little interest" or is "only of value in junior classes".

The failure of R.I. to do the job it is expected to do in transmitting the dominant ideas of orthodox Christianity to the new generation is no doubt related to the fact that the staffs of schools are themselves divided in their acceptance or rejection of these formerly dominant ideas. Over the years, morality based on religious sanctions has been giving way to morality grounded in convictions about what human relations ought to be and what our obligations to one another as human beings are. This humanization of moral outlook has spread among teachers as well as in society as a whole. A survey of the opinions held by over 600 students training to be teachers ten years ago showed an almost 50/50 division between those who felt that their moral choices were controlled by their religious convictions and those who felt they were controlled by human considerations. Such ideological division must exist in all schools that are not denominational schools. This, coupled with the expectations of the 1944 Act, produces a climate of pretence. It is a sinister factor in the confusion in so far as many teachers—25 per cent of those who filled in the questionnaires for *Religion In Schools*—feel that to declare oneself of unorthodox views may be a hindrance to professional progress. Section 30 of the Education Act ostensibly guards against this, but the fact remains that anyone appointed to a headship is legally responsible for maintaining religious instruction and worship in his school. Consequently, many heads feel obliged to assume a mask of conformity that belies their real convictions.

The schools are also faced with a curious hotchpotch of moral ideas that the children acquire from their contact with mass media. These are picked up partly by identification with hero figures from the worlds of show business and sport, partly from the content of plays and films they watch, and partly from advertising. For example, girls frequently acquire the idea that to be beautiful and desirable are the chief virtues of women and the surest guarantees of a happy life. The influence of screened drama shows clearly in a research into moral judgments carried out recently among a sample of junior school children by Dr M. L. Kellmer Pringle and J. B. Edwards. The children were asked to list "morally wicked actions". Kidnapping was included by 6 per cent of the children and blackmail by 3 per cent—hardly ideas that would occur to junior school children from their everyday lives.

This content of injected ideas the schools have to evaluate and guide as best they can. They can only do this by bringing moral education right into the arena of modern life as experienced by the children in their charge. Many teachers are prepared to do this because today's teachers are much more of the world than were teachers of a few decades ago. The pity of it is that some teachers feel under an obligation not to admit it and so sacrifice one of the surest links between themselves and the younger generation.

The crux of the matter is that the schools are in a false position. Society is at present engaged in a moral debate during which some formerly dominant ideas will recede, other ideas replace them, and then blend with the traditional ideas that survive the era of transition to cohere into a new set of dominant ideas that are both appropriate and acceptable to modern man. The schools should be taking part freely in this debate and so creating within themselves a lively climate of moral inquiry and interest. Instead they are firmly shackled to a traditional orthodoxy.

The debate is not primarily one of science versus religion but of discovering common ground. At a time when theologians are rejecting outmoded God concepts, scientists are penetrating so far into the nature of things that the mystery of existence becomes more baffling than ever. Indeed, Christian orthodoxy is now beginning to look like an oversimplification of something infinitely more mysterious and complex than our fathers supposed. What could be more evocative and exciting than participating in this debate?

Thus, our social efforts to assure the moral education of our young people through the requirements of the 1944 Act have become self-defeating. There is an urgent need to find an alternative to this abortive initiative. By all means let us start the school day with an assembly, and by all means let us see that the children know about Christianity which has had such a powerful influence upon the form their society has taken. We must dissociate the religious content of the curriculum from an assumed special role of Christian orthodoxy as the supreme instrument of moral education. So long as this role is assumed, R.I., far from assisting moral education, must inhibit it because teachers will be tempted to "leave it to R.I.". We should note that a change in approach to moral education, although it is needed throughout the school years, is particularly necessary at adolescence because it is a part of adolescence both to challenge and to search.

Of course, beneath the surface of conformist morality in our schools, the debate is in full swing. The question of behaviour between the sexes is a case in point. It is going on, with eager sincerity, among the adolescents and young adults of every school and college. But the formative value of this discussion is largely lost so long as teachers and others in authority feel obliged to propagate the orthodox Christian line. In place of frank discussion, we get a we-and-they conflict, with the rigid righteous on one side and the bulk of modern youth on the other. This impedes the emergence of moral clarity. The "crime" that Dr Peter Henderson committed in his now notorious speech last month before a group of teachers resides simply in his having stated that reappraisal of the human love relationship is in progress. Sir Edward Boyle has taken the truly educational line on this by saying that, so far as he is concerned, the debate continues. But dead ideas and a host of inconsistencies blot effective progress in moral education.

What, then, is the way forward? We must start by accepting that we are in an era of moral change and that the dominant ideas about man and his destiny that served their turn for several centuries are in process of giving way to other ideas.

One element of the moral change of the recent era is that the morality of obedience to external absolutes is being replaced by the morality of involvement and discovery. This gives pain to some people who seek rigid rules of thumb for the guidance of their lives. Yet those who still seek absolutes are themselves making selections and modifications in terms of social necessity. The second and fourth commandments are ignored as entirely impracticable. The seventh is often expanded to include all extra-marital intercourse; and the ninth to include lying in general. Some of the greatest moral problems in the world today—what to do about the population explosion, for example —are not catered for by the commandments. The absolutes of the past can have only a partial application to the changing present and lose thereby their status as absolutes. Within and between the Churches this has been shown by their readiness to consider reunification. They divided over disagreements about what was the absolute truth; they are coming together again because their particular beliefs have lost their absolute authority. Thus we are faced today not by problems of application in terms of absolutes but by problems of searching out a satisfactory moral basis for personal life and for society. The search is itself the moral education. It is a search in which all young people are ready to join, as anyone who has worked with adolescent groups is well aware.

Then, we must offer Man for moral study, not among the vestigial remains of Old Testament mythology—as a creature fallen by his own perverse will and despicable because of it—but in his true context, that of evolution, biological, psychological and social. The truth of evolution, and man's ability to play a constructive part in it, is the most inspiring fact that has dawned on the human intellect for hundreds of years, yet children can pass through ten or more years of education without being made aware of their stature and responsibility in the context of the creative process. At best, a little attention may be given in general education in the sixth form to evolution as an individual involvement and responsibility. The concept of evolution is one of the new dominant ideas and warrants a central place in education. It has moral leads in many directions. Man as a conscious participant in a universe-wide creative process is a more inspiring moral concept than man as a miserable sinner.

Once the illusion of absolutes is out of the way and the concept of man as a creative agent is included in our thinking, we are in a position to bridge the destructive conflict between those who set most store by a scientific explanation of events and those who prefer a religious viewpoint. Movement from both sides towards a common area of agreement has been going on for some time. Otherworldliness has given way to the belief that the job of humanity is to do something about life on earth here and now. Both scientific and religious viewpoints are, today, humanisms. But neither is only a humanism because each accepts that existence itself is shrouded in mystery. Each may wish to put something different into that mystery. One group may put a personal God there; the other a question mark; but each will agree that the ground of man's being is humanism within a mystery. This is the new starting-point. It provides a vast unifying common ground in terms of human involvement and purpose. This kind of background is what the young most need if their search for moral clarity is not to become bogged down in apathy and confusion.

A. D. C. Peterson, Director of the Oxford Department of Education, has pointed out that many subjects should have their place in moral education. All subjects are about humanity and human discovery, and all carry within them questions of integrity in human terms.

Many schools, dissatisfied with the moral tone created by a rule-ridden authoritarianism, have made the acquisition of moral insight by the pupils their specific aim. Some teachers of English, history and geography are careful to foster the moral insights that their subjects provide. More and more schools are incorporating within the curriculum discussions of problems of personal life—possibly the surest road to moral insight for adolescents. Some study social problems also. Yet, speaking generally, moral confusion is more characteristic of our schools than moral clarity. The approach of the 1944 Act has failed. There is no evidence to show that the incorporation of compulsory R.I. in the curriculum has had any positive impact whatever on the moral health of schools and nation. We have to think again.

9

The Help of an Adult

M LAUFER

19 DECEMBER 1963

Understanding the behaviour of young people may demand a readiness to forego the privilege of moralizing. Yet, there are many young people who feel troubled by something, and genuinely want the help of an adult. They do not want to be told that they are bad or evil, or that they should not worry about anything because they will sooner or later grow out of it. They want help in making sense of feelings about themselves, their parents, their friends, their future plans. At the same time they want to feel that the neutral adult can add another dimension to understanding these problems. Something which sounds incidental to the adults may be felt by the young person as a crisis—the opposite, too, can well be true. The adult who claims to be able to help must also demand certain things of himself: the ability to differentiate behaviour which is within the realm of normality from that which is a sign of more serious mental disturbance; the ability to see the problem as it affects the life of the person presenting it; the ability to treat the young person with respect.

When the Young People's Consultation Centre was opened in Hampstead two years ago, it was the intention of the officers of the Youth Studies and Research Foundation to create a service for young people between 15 and 23 where they could have the opportunity to talk with a professionally trained person about anything with which they felt they wanted help—be it career, accommodation, difficulty with boy- or girl-friend, difficulty at home, or the more serious emotional disturbances which may become manifest at this period. It was planned from the beginning that the Centre would be based on psychoanalytic principles. Four professional people, each trained in psychoanalysis or psychotherapy and with previous experience in social work, were appointed to be available on three evenings each week. The service is free, procedure about appointments is kept to a minimum, there is no waiting list, and confidentiality is completely assured. A psychiatric adviser and a medical adviser are available when necessary.

Our experience to date at the Centre has been an eye opener. Nearly 200 young people have attended during these past two years. They have come from all parts of London and the outskirts, from every social class, and from every educational and work group. The number of times a person is seen varies from once to five or six times, except for the small group of people who need long-term help. A large number of them see the Centre as a place to which they come just to talk over something which has been troubling them. Others are much more worried about their present emotional difficulties, and wish us to arrange for more long-term help. There is another group who need time and our help in accepting that their behaviour is a sign of disturbance which needs to be taken more seriously. There are, of course, some with whom we fail.

The stated problem for which a person comes to the Centre to seek help usually tells us very little. One person may be upset by some immediate crisis, e.g. loss of job, family difficulties, and so on, but will be able to handle this on his own without too much difficulty. A second person may make the same crisis into something which he sees as unmanageable, and may suddenly feel that nothing is any longer worthwhile. It is only after we have been able to fit the stated problem into the context of the whole life of the young person that we are able to know how to view what we are presented with. It is not enough to assume that A represents one thing and B another. Assessment of the problem, and deciding what is needed, are our immediate tasks. Unless the professional person has the training and experience to see the problem within a wider context, there is the danger of mishandling and misdiagnosis. This could be as harmful to the young person as could the attitude of "don't worry, you'll grow out of it", or "pull yourself together". It is mainly in this area that good intention on the part of adults can be harmful rather than helpful.

Every young person believes that his feelings, his worries, and his uncertainties are mainly confined to himself. When he comes to the Centre and explains what he wishes help with, he does not want to be confronted by an adult who looks surprised, or annoyed, or blank. He expects us, and rightly so, to take him seriously, and to try to help find an answer both to the immediate worry and to the meaning that this worry has for his future life. Since it has usually taken a great effort to decide to come to the Centre, he does not want to be told that he has come to the wrong place and that his problem would be understood better somewhere else. When he needs legal advice we arrange it for him, even though our main function is to get at the underlying causes for his behaviour.

We now have a small additional budget available so that some of the young people in need can be offered psychotherapy or psychoanalysis over a longer period of time. In these instances, our procedure is simply to offer them sessions with a qualified psychoanalyst or psychotherapist. The Centre guarantees the fee for this, and the young person contributes whatever he is able to.

In the course of setting up and enlarging the work of the Centre, we have been confronted by a number of problems outside our immediate scope, but which nevertheless are serious reflections of the community's attitudes regarding understanding and helping young people. We have often been asked why the Centre was set up in the first place, or why so much money is being spent on something which is already being done by other organizations. The answer to this is that this service is not available elsewhere. There is no organization where a professional person is available to talk to any young person who comes in. Clinics and hospitals are not meant primarily for the young person. Most young people are very hesitant to go to a hospital for help or advice because of their feeling that this would confirm for them that they are ill. Such services as do exist are numerically inadequate.

Another aspect which some adults find difficult to accept is the slow, cautious, and painstaking manner in which we work. Could we not shorten interviews, or just give advice, or collect information and see trends? Some people still believe that all that is needed by young people are the facts, and then all will be well, or that the young person should be taught to be nice to other people or to respect their elders. All these attitudes simply reflect the gap which exists between what some adults think the young person needs and what the young person is actually seeking. We are much more concerned about what the young person really feels than what adults think the young person should feel. The danger in cutting corners is simply that we would fail in understanding the needs of the young person, and we could fall into the trap of making available what we think they should have rather than what they need and want. We have tried to discourage the belief that a person must think he is ill before coming for help.

There is still a great deal to know about the emotional development of young people, and about the means of being able to help with both internal and external problems. The Centre has the unique opportunity of working with a large number of people who come with a variety of immediate problems and from a variety of backgrounds. Only by the slow process of interviews will we learn more about how young people actually live, and how we can be more effective in offering help. It is our intention to use the data available to broaden our understanding of the problems with which young people are confronted, and to study some of the technical factors which enter into work with people in a setting such as that of the Centre. Together with this, our experience may give other organizations the impetus to re-examine some of their approach which is considered established practice, but which may nevertheless be out of touch with the young person.

10

The Multi-racial Puppets

PIPPA PHEMISTER

18 MARCH 1965

I was, 20 years ago, a graduate in French, but I have often worked as a supply teacher. So I was not surprised when a Kilburn headmaster to whom I was sent last January asked me to replace a domestic science teacher. As he said: "Surely, if you've got a family of six children you can teach domestic science." Mentally admitting years of culinary botching, I refused. "Weaving? Basketwork?" I shook my head. Such pastoral crafts would be very unwelcome in Kilburn, even supposing I knew anything about them. "Puppets?" I suggested. "Puppets!" he seemed pleased. "That was my hobby in *my* youth! I shall be able to keep an eye on you!" It was too late to retract.

Hawkesbury Road Secondary Modern was a small school; about 300 boys and girls. Very few O levels. There was a lot of race friction in the school; white children were outnumbered, and resented the fact. I was now in a redbrick building which looked like a village hall built to commemorate the Boer War, and scattered with stainless-steel sinks and white gas stoves, large, empty cupboards and masses of tables and chairs. At the far end four girls were gossiping and making Nescafé. Yes, they were always there; yes, all day: for the staff.

My first class clattered in at 9.45: 25 adolescent girls. Six were black, three were mulattoes, one appeared to be Chinese, and the rest were an assortment of Italian, Cypriot, Irish, Turk and English. They were all vigorous and well fed. Many wore adult shoes that made them teeter. They ignored me, and quarrelled about who should sit with whom, and at which table. No one would sit at the same table as the black girls, not even the mulattoes. No one would sit with the mulattoes either. The Latins kept cagily to themselves. The Irish hissed "Jungle! Jungle!" if a West Indian approached them. The Kilburnese just screeched "Black Ape" at the Chinese. I thought, how patient the West Indians were: then the heftiest Negress heaved a wooden stool across the room, accidentally hitting a neutral Cypriot on the head.

When they wearied of this minor race riot the Chinese girl asked what we were going to do. Puppets. Puppets! Their disbelief and derision were boundless. I felt ashamed of myself for suggesting it, and lectured them huffily about puppets and their history. Even though clay puppets had been found in prehistoric Chinese tombs, they remained unimpressed. "But", admitted the Irish girl, "Television's got puppets!" "Yes", said the Chinese one, "It got Fireball . . ." They yielded. What else was there to do? They dozed off morosely in between their bickering about race and status. I was able to talk about what interested me to an audience that couldn't get away.

The Plasticine arrived; crates of it, all in primary colours. They tore at it, pummelled it, and their tempers improved. They even forgot sometimes and sat down at the same table as a Negress or a mulatto. Then they covered the Plasticine heads with *papier mâché*. Everything was covered in glue, newsprint, Vaseline and spit. When they found they had modelled a mask of Ringo or Cilla Black, they were delighted. They began to paint their masks. They dried them in the gas ovens. I brought a tape recorder, and we had music while we worked. They tried to be supercilious; but they were enjoying themselves.

Then the boys began to drift in. The reason I had no males to teach was that my rusty, married discipline was thought to be too weak to control them. But as their presence was clandestine I didn't need any discipline. If they were a nuisance I threw them out, but they were quiet. It was the professional trouble makers who came first. They were bored and frustrated in formal classes, and no one apparently missed them. The girls, flattered, began to teach the newcomers.

Mods and Witches

Rows of puppet heads now watched us from their wooden stands. We had false eyelashes, glassy eyes, glossy nylon hair by the hank and sumptuous materials for the puppet bodies—each body a glove scaled to the hand of the child who was going to work it. Each child decided what his puppet was going to be. Of course, we had the Beatles, Mods, Spacemen, Rockers and Winston Churchill. There was the occasional Nurse or Crinoline Lady. At the end of a month the magic beings, the people that last, began to emerge: knights, princes, kings, wizards, mermaids and witches.

The child wears his puppet—he cannot dissociate himself from the doll. He articulates head and ears with three fingers, body movements with the wrist and palm of his hand. This identification of child with puppet cuts across all barriers and categories, even sex. I was astounded when a very feminine, biddable Italian girl chose to work our fiercest dragon. She worked him ably, by herself, in a corner. When interrupted she suddenly took a heavy satchel and beat up a large boy who wanted her puppet. She *was* the Dragon, all fire-eating aggression and sullen threat. For the first time in her adolescent life she relaxed into what she really was. Another docile Kilburn youth, Dennis, sulked for three days because his mates would not allow him to work a mermaid. It was unthinkable, a mermaid was a girl. But he persisted, and his mermaid sang nostalgic folk songs, combed her flaxen hair, dived into our woven sea and coiled voluptuously round cardboard rocks. This time criticism was silenced. After all, that's what a mermaid is for.

Now we needed a theatre. Four Irish boys who were "playing up" in carpentry were seconded to bang and saw and cut their fingers and swear. At the end of a week we had an enormous puppet theatre, solid, elegant and eight feet tall. It towered above us like an assertion of wealth, papered in maroon and gold paper so expensive that I would have shivered to buy it for my own home. It had maroon brocade curtains, electric light and it worked. Here was the Best, waiting for them. Social rejects: they could see, use, be part of and live it. They began to squall less, and their spirits to revive.

The magic of the theatre began to work. It provided a total disguise for timid or inhibited people. If you put on the clothes of a king you become to some extent a king, whether you wish to or not; and in puppetry the release is total. Dress a Negro as a king and he is, at best, a Negro king. His black face and long legs cannot be written off. In the puppet theatre he can be any kind of king he wants. Similarly an ugly child cannot be turned into a beautiful princess on an ordinary stage. In puppetry her unwieldy body can be discarded while she *is* her puppet. Many nervous and downtrodden girls assumed assurance.

Everything in these children's lives was ugly and ineffectual. Their outlook on life was muddied and without purpose, and the possible, for them, was drab and limited. Puppet theatre, with its potential for *total* fantasy, gave them hope. On a stage you cannot turn the leading lady into a bat, or make a witch fly. But such basic metamorphoses are what humans in limited circumstances so bitterly desire. Puppet theatre makes the possible world without limits. The children began to relax.

The talents of the children were all the stronger as they had been untapped by the circumstances of their lives. They wanted formal dialogue and plays, and comprehended adult lines, and no elaboration of acting techniques seemed beyond them. While they wore the glove they *were* the puppet. This I first noticed when I was rehearsing a scene where a Prince goes to sleep on a sandy shore. While he sleeps, ignored by the audience for about five minutes, three mermaids come out of the sea and monopolize the stage. I concentrated on the mermaids' singing. Suddenly I noticed that the ignored Prince Puppet was breathing as he lay on the sand. He snored faintly as his "chest" expanded and contracted. Inside the glove the puppeteer's hand moved smoothly to give this effect, indifferent to anyone's noticing it.

TOTEM POWER

I called the power of the puppets totem power, to the children. The Negroes felt it most acutely. "Shango!" breathed one Port of Spain boy as he slipped a magnificent, glaucous green Sea Wizard into his hand. "Mama Lou, me, boy, Mama Lou, Me!" chanted a stout Negress who had that very morning slapped the young constable's face at our school crossing. Now she was a court lady. She stroked the masses of tulle streaming from her jewelled steeple hat. She bowed graciously to an admiring audience. She was all delicacy and *noblesse oblige*. But also, under the spell of the puppets, the Negro children became the bosses, let others introspect, shriek for help, sing songs or be rescued. They always played the dominant roles: princes with Swords of Atomic Puissance, dragons whose very breath could melt a battalion. They decided what course a play should take. If I forestalled them by writing a formal play they seized the dominant roles. And from the white children who would not share a pencil with them there came no murmur of protest.

Identification with the puppets was complete. If I snapped at a child for shoddy acting it was his puppet who told me to shut up. After all, I couldn't take a puppet seriously, however rude it was. Or could I? By this time I was as confused as they were. I noticed that one boy, normally a stammerer, was fluent as a puppet. I thought to record each child's ordinary conversation, and then its puppet dialogue. One of my best actors was playing the Deathly Moon Wizard. But as he was a six foot Negro boy he was lying on the floor of the theatre in a comfortable position, holding his puppet aloft, giving more acting space to the other puppeteers. His voice was consequently muffled. "Speak up, George," I said, feeling that he wasn't illustrating my point. But he was. For I was holding the microphone near the *puppet's* head. "You're going balmy!" sneered a blonde girl. "They'll come for you with the ambulance. Any time now, I should say. Puppets is getting real to you!"

They were. I took our best puppets home every evening because they were such a temptation to theft. When I unpacked them they still seemed invested with the quality of their children. A used puppet had much more personality. In Sicily the puppets that are owned as heirlooms by single families become similarly invested with personal power; it becomes in some obscure way animate.

The children responded to this sense acutely. What the puppets said, went. As the use of puppets undoubtedly strengthened the identities of all the children, race friction should have increased. In fact it lessened. The deposed, like myself, were too confused to mutiny. The new rulers were content to bask in power rather than abuse it. The hall became a club, with the hard-won privilege to get in where the puppets were. Everyone became infected with the notion that here was a world where usual laws did not obtain. It affected me. I began to wear trousers in class, and to smoke.

RELIEVING ALIENATION

It is so easy for a secondary modern school simply to reinforce the predictable squalor of thought usual in poor homes. The children, and the teachers, become content with what ought to disgust them. Many children in secondary modern schools are of grammar school intelligence, but are sapped of initiative, perhaps by illness, or by domestic inertia or hostility. Further demoralized by the fact of failing to go to grammar school, they then, as it seemed to me, were graded into

A, B or C streams in terms of relative disciplinary nuisance. The C stream was kept together to avoid disturbing the other children, and other teachers were delighted when my puppets attracted the C stream; but when A stream children were equally attracted the teachers were angry: good pupils were wasting their time! But in fact since hardly any O levels were taken at Hawkesbury Road the older children passed their terms in a haze of boredom, aware that whatever they did they were wasting their time. At least the puppets were interesting.

The more alienated a child was from his surroundings the more intense his relief, and performance, was in puppetry. This was illustrated by the case of Flanagan, Irish, handsome, C stream, an amiable nuisance. Some teacher had appointed him milk boy, which solved his educational problems. Milk is lugged around state schools in large, metal crates, on metal trolleys. What caretakers' sense of caste forbids them to do with the milk crates has to be done by the children. So Flanagan, and two Negro henchmen of robust strength and frail intelligence, spent their entire day doing obscure things with the milk, which was distributed by them throughout the school. After our milk crates had been delivered, Flanagan and his mates used to sit and watch us for an hour every morning. He seemed so silent and absorbed that I offered a puppet to him. He shook his head. "Not that one", he said firmly, "I'd like the Black Knight." He put on the glove and vanished into the theatre. There were no titters or jeers as there might well have been had Flanagan tried to do anything else for the first time. He had chosen for his glove the death-dealing Guardian of the Frozen Moon Shore. The curtains parted. Flanagan had vanished. He knew his part perfectly. But his voice was Irish and as ashen as the backdrop. He *was* death craving, death-dealing Ireland. He was medieval pageantry and metallic menace, black velvet of cloak and voice alike. He fought and died for his Moon Shore, mourned by his beloved dragon. The children and I sat and wept and blew our noses. Afterwards, the milk delivery service was raced through in three-quarters of an hour. Flanagan went from strength to strength, but later, alas, became an assistant in a supermarket.

Inside the tiny theatre children elbowed and shoved and swore and tried to eat the odd ice lolly while they were waiting for their cue. Physical segregation was impossible. However, outside race friction reached a new intensity. The usual small riots became increasingly vicious in intent and result. Canings and injustices were commonplace; the headmaster seemed neither surprised nor shaken. Evidently this was the usual pattern. Then during the last week of term a young Negress was bent backwards over a radiator and beaten with umbrellas by a multi-racial group of hooligans. Her spine was injured and she was taken to hospital. "It's no good, Mrs Phemister", the head said. "You can't do it. You're mixing them in too much. Not just the nigs— *all* of them. They're getting above themselves. How can we keep them where they belong if you treat them like this? Everyone's paying for all this matiness. It's not fair to the older teachers—makes *their* lives difficult, does far more harm than good. You're giving these people wrong ideas."

That afternoon I watched, with three other sympathetic younger teachers, our play for the last time. We watched the boy from Antigua put on the trappings of Prince Firebrand. We watched him rescue the Sun King's Daughter—an intrepid puppet played by the highly eligible daughter of a Kilburn Cockney who kept an all-night café down the road. It was the dress rehearsal. We watched the Princess kiss Firebrand's hands out of love and gratitude because he had rescued her from the Moon Wizard. The charming young man who taught carpentry put a consoling hand on my shoulder. "Never mind, Pippa. It's a beginning. Today it's the puppets. Tomorrow it'll be the puppeteers."

11

The Biggest Years in a Boy's Life

ROBIN GUTHRIE

17 JANUARY 1963

AUTHOR'S NOTE

I was greatly helped in this enquiry by Nick Hallings-Pott, who carried out a number of interviews.

Almost within living memory a man was prosecuted in Liverpool for allowing one of his cows to trespass on the first floor of a house in Upper Parliament Street. The road is now a main artery through some of the worst slums in Europe and the cows are many streets away; but though there are no fields, the spaciousness of a wealthy Victorian suburb has not been entirely blocked in. The houses are set back a little from a wide pavement, and the traffic moves freely and fast on the carriageway. From the top, especially at night, the road has the exciting feel of a thoroughfare in a European capital; its lights slope and loop away to plunge out of sight by the cathedral into the city and the docks. Many of the doorways have fluted columns and Ionic capitals; some are built in handsome Palladian terraces, their white plaster fronts contrasting with the grey-red brick of the rest. The people who built them for their houses have left now for Southport or the Wirral, and the present occupants make a strange mixture. Walk down Upper Parliament Street at night: Indians, West Indians, English, Irish,

Chinese and other nationalities move up and down so that a summer evening has the air of a *passagio* in a Mediterranean town.

The boys of the club in Upper Parliament Street have recently painted their premises, and every evening the light falls into the road over cheerful cream and maroon. Inside, shabbiness is banished; there are new banister-rails, new wallpaper, new paint, and vivid murals in the table-tennis room. The visitor to a club is at a disadvantage; little of the club's life appears on the surface, and it looks at first as though the life of the streets outside has simply moved within four walls; boys move around without apparent restraint, coming to the counter for a table-tennis ball or a Coca-Cola, or playing billiards, or watching TV; or they just stand and talk and scuffle.

Low Hill, a mile or two from Upper Parliament Street, is less dramatic; it lacks contrasts. Plunging streets of slums, bombed sites, rubble; pubs, dirt and kids—you either live on where you were born or you get a good job and move out. The houses are condemned, and everybody knows everybody else—there are no newcomers. Here, too, there is a club: boys of all ages pass in and out all evening—in to the pleasant wallpaper and the rough kindness of the warden, for table-tennis, or chess or billiards or TV; out to run wild in the streets.

Results are not easy to gauge in social work. Even the most convinced and dedicated club leader can doubt the value of his work. If we understood more about what we are doing, we might be able to do the job better and more confidently. "Permanent value", however, is not a matter for statistical analysis or factual report, and very little research has been done on the lasting results of Boys' Club work. I was commissioned in September 1961 to meet and talk to ex-members of two clubs in the areas of Liverpool which I have described. My brief was to try to discover from the horse's mouth the difference it makes to belong to a boys' club.

The task was obviously impossible. The value of a club is not subject to measurement. We who asked the questions were biased in favour of clubs. As for the men we interviewed, the individual is not the best judge of where and how his education took place; these men, moreover, were unused to thinking in concepts and to expressing ideas. Their horizons are narrow and their experience limited. It was difficult to draw anything out without first feeding in the kind of thing one was looking for. Furthermore, their minds do not move logically from one fact to another, or from a set of facts to a conclusion. For instance, a group of 14 men with whom I drank quantities of beer were enthusiastic even at the sober start about the club they had belonged to together, and gave explicit and spontaneous reasons; yet to the question whether or not they would send their own sons the most positive answer was "Oh, I suppose so". Reason is not a factor.

In spite of these difficulties we struck genuine and instructive feelings. The only real exceptions were, significantly, four very young ex-members, who criticised the facilities roundly. My mind went back to them when a man who had joined during the war said: "We were grateful for anything in those days."

Few had considered the nature or the quality of the facilities. They knew, however, why they had joined a club. All 44 were attracted in the first place by the opportunities for sport—several claimed that the club was their only opportunity of playing games. The majority remained interested only in sport; one or two took a real interest in some of the other activities (especially woodwork and drama), and most took part in them. One who is now a youth leader said: "It's a good idea to get boys into a club with football, but you've got to give them a lot more when they're in."

This appears to be contradicted by the fact that apart from football only two claimed to have kept up any activity learnt at their club (woodwork, boxing and basketball). The lapse seemed unimportant: what they felt *was* important was the variety of opportunities when they were growing up.

"What did you join for?" was one of the few simple questions that we could ask. Our conversation depended on the men being forthcoming about what they thought they got from the club. We tried to discuss such matters as the kind of influence they felt the club had on them as members, the effect of their membership on their present attitudes and outlook, their opinion of the value of clubs for the youth of today, and the part played by the leader of a club. About a dozen of the men we interviewed were inarticulate and unresponsive, as far as we could make out, to ideas of this kind. A few were aware of what we were getting at, but could not express themselves definitely: one, for instance, was convinced that ex-members of any boys' club could be distinguished in a crowd ("You only have to look"), but found the distinguishing characteristics impossible of definition. The majority produced clear and apparently spontaneous ideas. The warmth of their speech and their determination to find words for what they felt cannot be indicated by statistical tables: description and quotation may give some impression of what we encountered.

It was fascinating in the first place to hear them talk of the wild, amoral life of the streets; of the excitement of the goods-yards at night; of picking fruit off barrows or moving lorries; and of the ease with which a career of delinquency and crime could begin. The often reiterated comment "keeps boys off the streets at nights" was never a mere cliché among men who had all been juvenile delinquents, undetected or caught. The club could become an object of warm emotion; one man spoke of a friend who ran up to him "radiant" with the news "I'm in".

The club spirit and the companionship meant a lot to them. Most recognized the leader's all-important part in creating this spirit, though some felt that the members were solely responsible (and so paid the leader the greater compliment). Club spirit was most apparent when I interviewed the group of 14 men, members of an old boys' football team. Once I had met it there I could recognize it under the surface of the remarks of individual ex-members. They spoke not so much like men who wear the same old school tie as like men who have been up Everest or through the Army's basic training together. It had been a unique experience for them, of corporate, close-knit activity, and it had made a deep impression. One said of his joining that it was "the best thing I ever did", and in emphasizing this he described as vital the feeling that "we belonged". Connected with this was the fact that "we did all the decorating". Even the least articulate found phrases such as "learning to mix" and "making friends".

A number felt that the club made a difference in the way they set about a job of work. They compared their own attitude with that of others, especially with that of younger workers who "go for the smoking and drinking: they think of nothing else", and are "looking for kicks, as they call it now". One said "You get a good outlook on your work from the club"—this applied particularly to "working with others". "You learn to do things the manly way . . . things have got to be done the right way, that's the beauty of it".

More significant, and more surprising, were the apparently spontaneous remarks about general behaviour and attitudes. The ones I now quote were made with conviction and show no signs of being second hand. Mick told a longish story of the time his younger brother got a black eye from another member. Mick was inclined to bash the fellow, since he was, as he put it, "cock of the club at the time". He went instead to ask the leader for redress, but got no satisfaction. He reckons he learnt from the conversation with the leader which took place that "If you could get along without fighting, that was better", and called the incident an example of the kind of "education" you got in a club (though I felt there was still a shimmer of regret that he hadn't bashed the fellow in himself). The influence of the leader and the educative effect of club life depended in his memory on things the leader said in the night-to-night running of the club. "You didn't notice at the time, but you could see, looking back, the words they used, what was behind it". This was echoed in the words of another man who said that a lot went on (in the way of influence and guiding) which "you didn't notice at the time". Others said of their experience that it made them "good mixers", "a better citizen"; that "it made a lot of difference to my outlook on life . . . put me on straight lines . . . a chance to improve yourself . . . educating yourself . . .". One conversation went briefly as follows:

> Them four years is the biggest in a boy's life, for broadening your education like, and you can tell the difference in club members from the others, you know.
> *Is that because they were in the club?*
> I think so. I mean, 14 to 18 is a tricky time, you know; you can go one way or the other.

There was a small group who looked back on their club years as, for instance, "the happiest years of my life", but who specifically denied any benefits beyond "keeping lads off the streets" and "giving you something to do". About eight of the men interviewed came into this group.

A boy's relationships with his friends and his relationships with the leaders are more likely to keep him in a club than any hopes he may have of being educated. "Making friends" was frequently given as a reason for belonging to a club, and we had some examples of the effects of the friendships in small groups which boys tend to form. Every man interviewed joined in the first place through friends, and almost every one joined with friends. One said it was hopeless to join a club except "with a gang"; the individual was not accepted straight away. The strength of these friendships, not always made in the club but always enriched and confirmed within it, cannot be overestimated.

They spoke often of their friends, both of those whom they still see regularly, and, as vividly, of those whom they now rarely meet. Friendships had sometimes been so strong and satisfying that whole groups had "got around to courting and that" comparatively late in life. One man saw an argument for mixed clubs in this; he had joined the army "not knowing a single girl", and considered mixed clubs would mean "getting to know girls the right way". Another, often mentioned by his friends as an example of this trend, recently married at the age of 35. Not all approved of the idea of mixed clubs, however; of those who had an opinion, 8 were in favour, and 13 against—the argument against being that girls would be a distraction from the masculine activities of a club.

The leader was naturally often mentioned. Three-quarters of our sample vigorously championed the leader's all-important part in the success of the club. The rest either thought that he didn't matter at all or felt that he helped but was not essential. Only two seem to have failed to know and be known by the leader; they remember him only as someone who occasionally ticked them off. Two others paid their leader the high compliment of crediting only the members for success: "We made it good". The possibility that the leader and the members might depend on each other in the making of a successful club did not occur to them spontaneously.

One of the few facts of club work that can hardly be denied is that the boy is likely to benefit from contact with an adult in the formal-informal atmosphere of club life; the fact that so high a proportion spoke in such unmistakable terms about their own leaders bears this out. They appreciated the help and advice a leader could give in specific situations—when you were looking for a job, or when in trouble (though one who had recently been helped into a job seemed to have forgotten the part the leader played); but their appreciation went deeper. One "dedicated" man was much praised: "He had a good job of his own and he *chose* to work for ——." "A man you could trust." "He had experience of things we hadn't." " We learnt a lot from the leader. . . . Some boys would talk more easily to him than to their own fathers." It matters whether the leader is "hard" or "soft". Each in his own way found words for his feelings, but more expressive than words was the reaction of each man to the name of the leader; in the pub, as soon as each man came in, I was introduced not by name but by my connection with their former leader, and at the mention of his name I was at once accepted. None of them had had any actual contact with the man for some ten or twelve years. The look on their faces—surprise, pleasure and interest mixed—was one I saw on many door-steps. In the case where the leader was still working in the neighbour-hood there were signs of continuing and valued relationships.

"Wastage" is a problem for youth workers; a third of the members leave after six months or less. Most of the men we met were successes of club life; only four spent less than four years in the club. One spent two years as a member; he is now on the dole, and had very little to say for himself or the club. He joined for the sport and did nothing else. Another spent one year, and enjoyed particularly the carpentry; but he was disappointed when his work was sold for club funds. His brothers were both scornful of boys' clubs and emphasized the need to do exciting things. Another member stayed for only a year because he joined late through not knowing about the club. The fourth stayed only six months; he joined with friends but only he achieved the club football team. His friends left and he followed. He was, all the same, enthusiastic about clubs and gave the address of his brother, who had spent several years in the same club.

None of these failures appears significant. In the course of the enquiry, however, we did meet a number of men who seemed to have benefited very little from club life. They joined for somewhere to go at nights, they played football, and in due course they left; and although they might look back happily on their years of membership we could uncover nothing which they might have gained of per-manent value. These were depressing interviews, as failures of human contact are always depressing. In our sample there were only five such men, but we were more likely to meet the successes of club life and the five were not untypical. Lack of responsiveness in the individual must account for a good deal of wastage; it prevents his involvement in the relationships and activities of the club. Some do respond, for the first time, to the stimulus of club life; one man joined only for the sport and took up other activities very unwillingly; then he became so keen that he missed his night-school classes and his chances of trade qualifications. (After three unsettled years he now has a good job.) Others simply hang around in the club until apathy or a rival attraction keeps them away.

Wastage of another kind concerns those boys who never join a club or who leave in a gang for the freedom of the streets. Sometimes the

12

Emancipated and Reactionaries

ALEC MACGUIRE

28 MAY 1964

The recent gang-style rioting between Mods and Rockers may have distracted our attention from some of the sociological characteristics of these two phenomena. A *Guardian* reporter on 18 May, the day after Margate and Brighton, referred to them as groups differing only in their style of clothing. Most other recent commentary has also referred to them as groups mainly distinguishable by their external characteristics. Although they may participate equally in many of the features of contemporary adolescent behaviour, enjoy the same music, dance with similar steps and choose clothing differing from that worn by the adult population in general, my feeling from personal observation is that there are vital differences between these two groups.

What no one seems in any doubt about is that we have recently seen something very different from the clashes of gangs as we usually define them. There have suddenly arisen two super-gangs, each defining the other as an out-group and each sufficiently identifiable to be a ready target for the other.

Perhaps these two groups are self-conscious developments of the slow and stupid Teds and the Italianate sharp kids of Colin MacInnes' *Absolute Beginners* of the late fifties. But MacInnes was writing about fringe groups, whereas large numbers of adolescents now appear to align themselves with the Mod-Rocker continuum, even if they describe themselves as Mids, Tickets, Individualists or Stylists. My guess about the technical school where I teach is that over half of the boys there between the ages of 13 and 18 identify themselves in some way with these groupings. In nearby secondary modern schools the involvement is said to be even more evident.

What is quite surprising is the vehement commitment of adolescents whom school are about to enter for up to seven subjects at O level. "I wish to God that when I wake up tomorrow there were no more Rockers alive" said an otherwise gentle fifth former. The same boy was certain that the development of the Mod "movement" (his word) has reduced the volume of juvenile delinquency; it was the Rockers who were responsible for juvenile crime.

Among the boys I teach the identification is expressed more clearly in terms of antagonism towards the out-group than of commitment to the chosen one. A self-styled Rocker wrote of the Mods: *Long sleek hair, expertly styled and lacquered. Gorgeously shadowed eyes with pencilled brows. Cherry-red lips standing out from the delicately powdered face. And that's only the boys!*

This is the main burden of the Rockers' criticisms of the Mods, that they are effeminate in style and behaviour. "A Rocker's girl expects him to protect her as a man should, but a Mod expects his girl to defend him", said another fifth former. "The Mods smoke tipped cigarettes and wear Hush-puppies", said another with scorn.

It is clear that Mod fashions for boys do contain a number of traditionally feminine features, beginning with the idea of fashions that are continually changing and can be followed through the medium of the fashion pages of magazines. Long hair, make-up and hair lacquer, clothes in bright colours and of flimsy materials and high-heeled shoes have in the recent past been regarded as feminine prerogatives.

This is something not altogether new nor confined to adolescents for, with the diminished importance of manual work, the increase of affluence and the development of new materials, men's clothing has been modified considerably in the last 20 years. Cosmetics in the form of deodorants, talcum powders, pre and after-shave lotions have long ago penetrated the male market. Colour and comfort have become the criteria of men's leisure wear and the uniformity of sports jacket, grey flannels, white shirt and best brown brogues has given way to a variety of forms of sartorial self-expression for all age groups. As far as hair styles are concerned "Short back and sides" has become *passé* for the middle-aged as well as the young in a period where the columnist of a week-end review advocates tipping the barber at least 2s. One could regard the Mod development as a rather headlong acceleration of an already ongoing process.

As the boys have stolen some of their thunder some of the Mod girls have attempted to achieve greater femininity, and at the Mod Ball which some 8,000 teenagers attended in Wembley in April long dresses and a great deal of decoration with buttons, bows, lace and frills were their response. On the other hand many of the advertisements for clothing aimed at the Mods illustrate complementary versions for "Him" and "Her".

Frequent references are made by schoolboy Mods to themselves as "Individualists" and a letter in a recent teenage publication objecting to the mass promotion of Mod symbols, reads, "I'm an Individualist now. That's what Mods were supposed to be before". There would seem to be an emergent relationship between the total Mod image and this stress on individuality, the amount of money available for spending on personal adornment and amount of exposure to education. In the C streams of grammar schools one hears more of Mods than Rockers, while the converse is true of the C streams of modern schools. Mods are more likely to have benefited from the educational system: some have reached O level and stayed at school after 16. Much attention has been drawn to the O level attainments of the Beatles who, according to a number of schoolboys, mark for them the beginning of the Mod development two years ago.

The Mods describe the Rockers as poor relations who cannot keep up with their own expenditure on clothing; as dirty, oil stained and smelly. The Rockers' expressed values about clothing are traditionally masculine; clothes are meant to be hard-wearing, especially for motor-cycling. The Rockers are very critical of the Mods' lightweight anoraks which began as scooter gear. Rockers regard themselves as mechanically capable, able to tune and repair their own motor cycles. They find self-expression easier in physical than in verbal terms. Their chosen vehicle-symbol, the motor cycle, is assessed in terms of physical performance rather than external appearance, as is the case with the Mod scooter with its various chromium adornments. "A Mod takes his scooter into the garage if the slightest thing goes wrong," said a fifth former derisively, "they are afraid of getting a bit dirty."

The Rocker appears to dominate his "bird" who is expected to ride pillion faithfully to one boy. He pays the expenses for outings and in exchange "gets what he wants" said one boy hopefully.

Great emphasis is laid on the co-operation between Rockers to make their machines more efficient and speedier. This is an emphasis on male solidarity that schoolboy Mods do not echo. This solidarity is expressed again in the greater identity of Rocker clothing—jeans, boots and leather jacket, compared with the individuality sought after by the Mods. Rockers, in fact, are a reactionary group representing traditional working-class attitudes: masculinity, male dominance, male solidarity.

While the Rockers taunt the Mods with effeminacy, the Mods describe the Rocker girls as "trying to look like men". They are also characterized as aggressive and the source of a great deal of the trouble between Mods and Rockers. A 13 year old explained that he was a Mod because there were more Mod girls than Rocker girls. An older boy said that "Mod boys only dance with Mod girls, but Rockers will dance with anybody".

The Rockers seem less well provided with literary support than the Mods, perhaps because they are less literate. At least five magazines that can be said to appeal to Mods have appeared since January 1964 at prices ranging from 1s for the weeklies to 2s 6d for the monthlies. The weeklies sell around 500,000, the monthlies 250,000 each, suggesting that Mods far outnumber Rockers. One of these is *Ready, Steady, Go*, a magazine related to the television programme which began as a programme of pop music to appeal to adolescents in general but which was rapidly "adopted" by the Mods. This programme was responsible for the organization of the Mod Ball.

Why was it that at Margate and Brighton it was the Mods that were on the offensive? It may be useful to distinguish two elements in the Mod/Rocker dichotomy: first, a status element where belonging to the "supergang" and actively participating in gang-style battles gives the individual a sense of personal achievement and, secondly, a role-component where self-definition in the primary sex role is achieved through reference to one group or the other. For some adolescents these super-gangs will perform the functions of the "gang" as usually defined, providing group membership for individuals who are often unacceptable to other groups on their own terms; for other adolescents they act merely as reference groups.

A far smaller number of adolescents will be of the kind that have in the past sought personal significance through gang-membership and were described at Margate as "petty little sawdust Caesars". One would expect the active and aggressive adherents of these two factions to be more nearly matched because of the tendency towards a balance of power in gang-warfare that Colin Fletcher has described (*New Society*, 20 February 1964). Therefore it would not be surprising to find that where trouble occurs between Mods and Rockers each group would from time to time represent the aggressor.

The clear perception of each group as an out-group on which can be projected adolescent fears and prejudices is a pregnant source of violence. Some of the stereotypes held have already been described. Secondary modern school girls regard the Mods as "dirty fighters" who fight with knives. The Mods are also typified as physically smaller. In the school in which I teach it was interesting to note the frequency with which the charge of "wasting time" was levied at the out-group. Both Mods and Rockers define the other group as the "troublemakers".

The status-seeking component in this phenomenon can be explained in terms of a long literature on the gang, but the role-definition element needs a great deal more explanation. Why the growing effeminacy in terms of external symbols? Why the harking back to the costumes and styles of previous periods? One of the most recent pop groups style themselves "The Pickwicks" and appear in Dickensian costume complete with top-hats. What are the personal characteristics of the adolescents most likely to accept Mods and Rockers as reference groups?

This cult of "individualism in unity" can hardly be a creation entirely of the advertising and merchandising world, though clearly considerable advantage is being taken of a large potential market for clothing, beauty preparations, records and other items for which adolescents are already heavy buyers. Why has the idea of being part of an identifiable but non-organized youth movement become popular enough to sell magazines related to it by the million? What are the qualities of its heroes and heroines?

What are the features of life for the modern adolescent from a variety of social and educational milieux that make agreeable this process of self-identification and the building up of unfavourable stereotypes of other adolescent groups? To what extent do self-con-

13

The Margate Offenders: A Survey

PAUL BARKER

30 JULY 1964

Using his magistrate's freedom, Dr Simpson called them petty saw-dust Caesars when they came up in his Margate court last Whit Monday. Another Bank Holiday is about to break, with a good chance of more teenage trouble at the coast. It is the right moment to check over the accuracy of that headlined phrase, and to see how many of the clichés about Mods and Rockers have any truth in them. A clear picture of the Margate invaders may dispel the emotion that will otherwise blur an accurate look at their presumptive heirs this coming week-end.

It could indicate, too, if there is any way to prevent these outbreaks, and what their underlying motives are. Every commentator at his Fleet Street or vicarage typewriter produces the same notions: boredom, bad schools, parents' laxity, broken homes, too much affluence, too much publicity. The words all trot out so easily. Have these truisms the merit of being true? *New Society* has carried out a questionnaire survey of the 44 young men and teenagers who came up at Margate on Whit Monday. All of them were found guilty and given sentences that varied from three months' jail to a conditional discharge. Ours was a survey in depth as we believe there is value in getting to know one group well. Some generalization is possible from the results, though it would be wrong to apply them too widely. One thing they suggest is

115

how lightly the group most likely to be influenced—the defendants' friends—took the sentences. It raises the whole question of what did Margate stop?

Thirty-seven of the group were charged with threatening behaviour; three of them also with possessing an offensive weapon. Five were solely on an offensive weapon charge. One (it was alleged) had caused actual bodily harm as well as carrying a weapon. One was charged with inciting a breach of the peace.

One got a 12 months' conditional discharge. One was fined £25; 30 £50; and 5 £75. Four were sent to a detention centre for 3 months; 1 for 6 months. Two got 3 months' jail. (These two were the only defendants over 21, apart from the man who was given the conditional discharge after saying he had protected his young daughter.)

All except eight pleaded guilty. Several of them told the interviewers that they did so because the police had advised them to. For others it was because it seemed to them that those who pleaded not guilty got heavier sentences. The strained atmosphere of a courthouse seems to have been responsible for this misconception. The bench gave stiff sentences all round. Many of the teenagers felt the sentences were unfair and that they had been brought to court on wrongful charges. Whatever the truth of that, it seems clear that both the court and the police were hoping for a deterrent effect.

The 44 appeared in front of the magistrates the day after the worst Margate trouble. On Monday the main focus shifted to Brighton. Brighton paused before trying offenders and did its best to reach the parents of anyone under 21. Margate sped things along. Parents of defendants over 16 weren't told. The mother of one 19 year old spent the whole night alone at home, worried sick about where her son was. He got a £50 fine after pleading guilty. (On appeal, at this month's quarter sessions, a retrial of his case was ordered, with a plea of not guilty entered.) Juveniles got more leisurely treatment, appearing at the juvenile court a fortnight later.

More than three-quarters of Whit Monday's defendants answered the full questionnaire for our interviewers. We saw the two who went to jail because they came out with full remission, but the five in detention (where remission is only a sixth of sentence) weren't out in time. One got a conditional discharge on appeal. Two teenagers refused to reply because of pending appeals (which brought them both orders for retrial), though the 19 year old I mentioned before gave some background information. Two boys had switched addresses and couldn't be traced. With only one did we get a point blank No—from his family. The final return was 34 questionnaires, plus the single more general statement which couldn't be analysed with our other answers.

Altogether the teenagers were very ready to talk, but their parents were less keen till they were sure it meant no further personal publicity. The big reason given for both reactions was the feeling that the sentences were unfair. Even allowing for a natural self-justification, it is remarkable that 20 of the codable answers to "Why did the police arrest you?" came down to "arbitrary arrest". Four people felt they'd been mistaken for a typical Mod or Rocker. Only six admitted they had been in any fighting. That group of 20 who thought their arrest was arbitrary claimed mostly to have been doing nothing, or else moving away from trouble, when they were arrested.

ARREST AND PUNISHMENT

One boy I interviewed myself is typical of this attitude. I think he was being honest; but if he were not, his view of the police would remain relevant. He and some other Mods had been playing "childish games" among themselves on the beach. There was no violence to this, he maintained, though he admitted that earlier some Rockers had been hit over the head with broken deckchairs. He had not been doing the hitting. As he was coming off the beach with a piece of wood in his hand that he had been kicking around on the sands, he tossed it on to a pile of rubbish by the steps. A policeman said: "Pick that up, laddie." "Like a fool, I did. He arrested me, and I was charged with carrying an offensive weapon." He could see that, faced with an apparent riot, the police needed to arrest somebody. That might have some effect on the troublemakers. But he didn't think he should have been up on this charge. He pleaded guilty in court because he felt it would be best to get it over with, and was fined £75 for this and threatening behaviour (his first offences).

That boy was still at grammar school, which shows how wide a scatter of people our survey netted. There was also the epileptic from a rehabilitation centre whose aggressiveness had taken him in and out of court ever since he was 10. The Margate police knew him as he used to live in lodgings there.

I met up with some of my old mates in Margate. The police kept moving us on, which we didn't like. One of my mates said to one of the police: "That uniform bothers me." We both had a go at the copper and my mate was arrested. Later on, I was arrested when I was trying to resist being pushed around by the police. Earlier on, we had had a few bundles with Mods. We had had a few drinks. I counted for about half a dozen myself. Usually there were several of us fighting against each Mod.

Was prison any more appropriate for him than a £75 fine for the other boy? For all except ten of our sample, it was a first "offence" that brought them to court in Margate. The average age of defendants was about 18, so these were not habitual delinquents. Twenty-two said they would make sure they weren't mixed up in anything like this again. Most gave their Margate punishment as the reason, or fear of worse next time. "The fine is 50 good reasons for not doing it again", a Mod said, who had had to find most of the money from his savings for clothes. But several cited their night in the cells as the worst part of the punishment: "I had to sleep on a stone floor, and I was only given two pieces of toast and a cup of tea in 25 hours." Or here is another first offender, a 19 year old apprentice printer: "I know what the police are like now. They arrest anyone."

There were still some who thought "It's a free country, I'll go to the trouble again if I want". One Mod has already been in a dispute with Rockers at Brighton since Whitsun. Two points on the south coast and one in East Anglia have been provisionally chosen as this week's jousting grounds. Our respondents' forecast will soon be tested. So will their belief that they are the only people likely to be put off from going. Some of them will be at other parts of the coast for the holiday. "Maybe I'll end up at Southend with my feet in the water." But at least one intends to "stay at home and watch all the other goons on the TV. They need their heads examined if they go after what they gave us at Clacton, Margate and Brighton". However, he assumed that they would go.

Whatever the recipients themselves thought of their punishment, their friends thought it "a great joke", or "they looked up to me after that". One 21 year old was given "a Beatle reception" by his mates when he came back from prison. At worst, friends thought the mistake had been to be caught. (Only the grammar school boy faced a split reaction. "My Mod friends thought it was great. My school friends said I was an idiot.") The deterrent effect of the sentences can hardly be wide. Another difficulty in deterrence is that each outbreak has been a pretty separate phenomenon. Only four of the Margate group had also been at Clacton. One had been to Brighton, but that was on the Friday: when the police moved him and his Mod friends on, they drove over to Margate.

Half the people we spoke to said specifically that nothing could be done to stop the kind of behaviour there was at Whitsun. "All Britain's teenagers do it." "When everybody is a teenager, he has energy he wants to get rid of." The rest had the usual mixture of suggestions: "Put them all in the Army" (a laundry hand); "It's because they have no other outlet. They should put up a battlefield and let them fight if they want to" (a car finisher); "Move in more police so there is more certainty of arresting the real troublemakers" (a hairdresser). They sounded just like the professional men in the street so often encountered by evening newspaper reporters.

A few said cut down on the publicity. But also no one admitted to getting the idea for going to Margate from television or the press. The recurrent source was friends. Publicity may have influenced those who went on Sunday, rather than Saturday or Friday, more than they said. But it would only be a reinforcement. Every teenager in south-east England appears to have known about Margate and Brighton beforehand. "I went to be in with the brethren: good old week-end sort of business." "People who didn't go wouldn't have any life in them." Only about a quarter admitted to expecting trouble. But it is significant that all of them are expecting trouble at this week-end's gatherings.

Some were genuinely at the Margate outbreak by accident. One lived there; five said they visited the resort regularly. A Midlands hosiery worker had booked a flat there with some friends three months before. He claimed not to know the difference between a Mod and a Rocker. He was arrested, he said, when "walking down the sands", which is "what you're there to do". Prudently, he is spending August Bank Holiday at Butlin's, Bognor Regis.

Only one person went to Margate alone. Everyone else went with at least one friend, or the intention of meeting up with friends there. One boy's face lit up as he described the Mod camp above Margate: it had been the event of his year. Another, from north London, said he knew about 100 people who were going. Large batches also went from the Peckham, Bromley and Chatham areas. Our own sample broke down into: east Kent 6; Medway 4; south-east suburbs 1; South Bank 5; north London 4; western suburbs 7; Midlands 2. So it wasn't wholly an outsiders' invasion. Publicity had some impact once people were actually at Margate. A young meat porter explained why he blamed the newspapers:

> By the railway station a cameraman asked "Give us a wave". So me and a group ran about and waved some flags we'd bought. My picture was in the paper. We were pleased; anybody would be. After that, I put the flag in my pocket and went down to the beach and got arrested. I'd only been in Margate 30 minutes.

The groupiness of Margate only reflected the way a normal week was spent. One Rocker who lived in digs was the only person to mention solo activity. "I've more time to think than most Rockers. As soon as they get home, there's a family screaming: 'Where have you been till this time?'" But he wasn't fond of his solitude. "Oh, yes, sure I'll marry. This is what'll drive me to it", waving a hand at the small room with its unmade bed. Of those who classed themselves as Mods or Rockers, the pattern of weekday evenings was fairly similar. They would be out every night but one—probably Wednesday, when cash was low. That night they would spend with the family; others were spent with friends, mostly the same group, usually all male. Girl friends are compartmented off from the main part of life. One boy takes his girl dancing at a rhythm and blues club, takes her home, then goes out with his mates.

On Saturday, it is work or home in the morning; shopping for Mods or a caff for Rockers in the afternoon; dancing in the evening. Home again for Sunday morning and afternoon, and a dance again at night. Rockers are more likely to slip an old-fashioned visit to the pictures in somewhere. Neither group watches television much. Mods listen to the radio rather more often.

Fourteen of our interviewees classed themselves as Mods (counting in the punctilious Peckham teenager who said it was all Stylists now: this subtlety hadn't yet reached suburbanites and provincials); nine were Rockers; and twelve said they were neither. A few of the mid-group aligned with Rockers, and one or two were outside the rivalry altogether. But to an interviewer's eye, the rest looked like Mods.

The mids were generally staider. With an average age of 19, they were a year nearer the oldies than the Mods and Rockers proper. They spent more time during the week with their families, while Mods and Rockers were out with the group. When they went out, Mods were slightly more likely to be at dance clubs than Rockers. ("Whenever I go to a dance hall it's all Mod," a Rocker mourned. "And as soon as I've learnt the twist and the shake, they're off on to something else that I can't do. I can only dance at parties.") But the main difference between the rivals was that one spent its time *being* Mod, and the other *being* Rocker. This doesn't mean that no Rocker knows any Mods, or vice versa. One teenager said how well he got on with the Rocker over the next door hedge. But that is only in odd moments.

The Mods and Rockers had a positive and a negative image of themselves: the positive revealed by how they saw themselves, the negative by how they saw their rivals. Both saw themselves mainly in terms of dress: either the well known smooth get-up of the Mods, or the leather jacket and faded blue jeans of the Rockers.

The negative images are different. Rockers see Mods as effeminate. "They can wear skirts if they like, so long as I don't pick one up as a girl": that was a tolerant opinion. Mods see Rockers as slovenly and dirty: "Long greasy hair—they use axle grease. They stink of petrol fumes." One mid who sided with Mods built in a defence against the expected accusation. "I've never come across a Mod with make-up, whatever Rockers tell you."

Neither group particularly defines itself by its attitudes, though one Mod said: "Mods can talk among themselves. Rockers just say 'Huh, gimme a cuppa tea'; that sort of thing." To which the comeback is: "Rockers have a healthier attitude to life. You won't find any drugs, and not much drinking." The Rocker outlook (for this boy) seemed to come down to straightforwardness and an overriding interest: "A Rocker has his motorbike. You'll find him talking or generally playing the fool, but mostly he dreams, eats and sleeps motorbikes." The point about the two ways of talking is this: Mods go in for sophisticated "chatting-up". Rockers are less articulate as a rule; and if articulate, they incline to old-style pubby "discussions".

That was one of the rare boys to define his group according to vehicle. This is less important than in the popular stereotype, though motorbikes are something of a group myth for Rockers.

BIKES, MONEY AND PARENTS

The reported invasion of Margate by scooters and motorbikes is exaggerated. Of our sample, only seven went by bike or scooter (and that included one mid). Thirteen used public transport, 12 went by car, and one hitched. The Rockers made more use of public transport than Mods.

"Rockers are poorer than Mods," one Rocker said. This was scarcely true. The average take-home pay of the whole sample was £11 a week, for Rockers £10. In our size of sample, it wasn't a significant difference. But it was significant that mids took home £13 10s. And it was true that Mods came from a rather better off background, and could look forward to steadier future earnings. "Mods are more likely to be learning a trade" was a more accurate statement. The typical Rocker had an unskilled manual job; the typical Mod was a semi-skilled manual worker. The Rocker's father was a semi-skilled worker; the Mod's was non-manual. The boys themselves did not remark on any distinction between them in terms of class, and the lines weren't rigidly drawn. Five Mods were unskilled. No Rocker had a non-manual or skilled manual job.

People joined the one group or the other, they said, because they liked that style of dressing, or because they despised the other style. "Mods are more like women" again. Some areas can be purely Mod or Rocker: not whole towns or boroughs, just an estate or a village, which can be enough to put pressure on a teenager through the boys he has as friends. This pressure doesn't always work. One boy from a drab Kent housing estate that was solid Rocker classed himself as a Mod. He had made outside friends, at art school rather than locally. Ever since taking a job in Cornwall when he was younger, he had wanted to "break away". He was 19 and a roofing labourer. A Mod apprentice printer from the western suburbs used to be a Rocker but "grew out of it". He now scorns Rockers as a bit moronic. There was no case of a Mod becoming a Rocker.

If clothes are so important, what did they spend on them? The answers we got are more valuable for what they tell about attitudes to fashion than for strict arithmetical accuracy. Two Mods said they spent

£25 the previous month; four Rockers had spent hardly anything. No Rocker claimed to have spent more than £12; no Mod less than £4.

Mods, Rockers and mids were all likely to have a record player, and somewhat less likely to have a transistor set. There were only three cars: fairly distributed into one for each group. No one was heavily tied up with hire purchase. The trappings of affluence had usually either been bought cash down or given as presents.

We must shoot down the broken home cliché as well. Only eight in the sample were not living with both parents. One son was living with one parent because the other was dead. In one case, both parents were dead; in another, both were abroad. The sole married man was living in digs with his wife and family. Only two cases were at all theatrical: with one parent dead and the other missing; and a 17-year-old Rocker more or less thrown out of home two years ago because he stayed out too late. Even so, he lived with his grandparents. The Rocker whose father and stepmother were abroad had a harder life. He is worth some detail—to guard against replacing the old rules of thumb by new ones.

His mother died when he was two. His stepmother was Jewish, his father was a foreman baker. They went on a trip to Israel two years ago and liked it so much they decided to stay. He hasn't joined them (he says) because of the cost of the trip, and "when it comes to it, you don't like to leave England". But before they left, he was already leading a pretty separate life. In the rooming house his father then ran, he had a top floor room where he could do what he liked. "My father said: provided I didn't bring the law in the house. And if I got a girl up the stick, I married her or he would break my neck."

He brings home just over £10 a week from a semi-skilled building job. He pays £3 a week for a single room. It cost him £1 a week to run his Thunderbird bike till he sold it because of the Margate fine. His room was hung with trophies: cowboy hats and spurs; drawings of James Dean, with dates of birth and death; buffalo horns fixed to bed head.

His attitudes were pleasantly traditional. He respected his "guv'nor" at work. "If there's anyone I'd like to grow up like, it's my dad." "Coppers aren't coppers any more. There are too many young fellers going around trying to be big." (Other respondents picked on this.) He spent a lot of time at Father Bill's—the vicar who runs the 59 Club for motorcyclists in Hackney. "You're always welcome. He's all right is old Bill." He sometimes got fed up with things, "but if I had a motorbike, I wouldn't be fed up. You can travel around, see life. With a bike you can travel from the East End right over to Golders Green. That's two different kinds of life. So you're not fed up". He liked to see different faces outside work.

"Last year I had my own gang. There were about 100 of us. We all went down to Margate then and had a great time in the arcades. We didn't hit any old ladies or smash any shop windows." This time he knew there was trouble in the wind. "But I didn't think it would affect us. I've always thought that if you stay away from trouble, it stays away from you." He deliberately left a bunch of keys and a studded belt at home. He gave me his explanation of how the Mods had provoked the Rockers. He showed me how to make the kind of improvised knuckleduster out of a newspaper and pennies that he had been carrying when the police picked him up.

Like other Rockers in the sample, he was more direct about toughness. He was more willing to admit he had been arrested for something genuine. But he complained: "The same brawl at the end of this street wouldn't have caused any bother. At Margate it was a big thing. It had to be glory." His own reading matter was mainly the *Mirror* and *Titbits* ("because the *Reveille* is so ropey"). His mind was sharp enough: "Why haven't I seen *New Society* at the newsagents? . . . Make it clear to me: is it a *Times* level of publication or a *Mirror* level?"

Most Mods and mids got fed up with the life they led, where one week seemed much like the next. The Rockers were less discontented. Mods would mutter about IQs. But they were no better than Rockers at suggesting alternatives to end their boredom. "There's not much you can do. No one wants to do anything like football." Either the alternatives were banal ("I'd like to go to the Discotheque") or more ambitious than the boy intended to achieve ("play around with vintage cars"). Hardly any belonged to any organization other than a dance club, though some of the exceptions were striking.

This low level of ambition, interspersed with aims that were presented as unattainable (hence not much better than daydreams), also characterized the answers to questions about work. Nearly everyone was very keen to go out to work. They tended to have a clear idea of the job they wanted: usually manual skilled. Many got it, though whether they liked what they had got was a different matter. Of those who failed to get the job they wanted, Rockers were more liable to be overfaced by the prospect of training or of breaking away from friends. There had been many changes of employer, but few of occupation. Only 9 people we saw had stuck to one firm, but 29 were in the same type of occupation as when they left school. Rockers often had more casual jobs, and so they had changed bosses most.

To the wide question "What would you like to do for the rest of your life?" the answers were revealing. Twelve wanted their present job; 9 a slightly higher position; and 11 a violent change. The meat porter wanted to be a Mayfair drinking club owner, the cook an airline pilot. So what job do you think you *will* do? The same as now: 21. Only one expected to achieve something really different: the cook thought he would make airline steward. The meat porter considered he would be "more or less labouring—that's all I am". (He made one of the very rare class conscious remarks. "If you ever want the views of a lower class teenager, get in touch with me.") Why these gaps between dream and reality? The replies became vague and implausible: "You need friends" to become a lorry driver. It would be some immovable obstacle like that: lack of money, perhaps, or fate. The dustman who got a Beatle reception after jail wanted to be "something useful which will do good: a probation officer." He expected to stay a dustman, however.

The idea of studying was offputting. Almost half had begun some kind of further education. Only three Mods were still attending. All but two had left school at 15. The grammar school boy hoped to stay on till he was 19 and go on to college, and a mid stayed at comprehensive school till 16. Three, altogether, had been to comprehensives—none of them Rockers, who were all secondary modern. The weight of the Mod sample tilted heavily towards liking school and finding the work interesting. In both groups, now they had left, there was a kind of sympathy for teachers; a surprising number of ex-pupils felt that the teachers had shown interest in both them and their work. The typical Mod and Rocker both claimed to have been in the top half of the class for sport. The Rocker was in the lower half for school work, the Mod was about average. (Mids, appropriately, were average in both.) However incorrect their own estimates may be, they are a good guide to how the groups felt they should have done at school (as distinct from now, when sport came nowhere with most of them). The typical Mod said his best subject was English, the mid said sciences (including maths), the Rocker crafts. (Three cultures?) There was little wide dissatisfaction with the schooling they had had. But a clutter of sensible remarks emerged about newer buildings, smaller classes and younger teachers, alongside a few mavericks like "better dinners" or "religious teaching is ridiculous". Not one reply mentioned the words 11 plus or comprehensive school.

Schools won't dissatisfy Mods and Rockers, work won't give them ambition, magistrates will find it hard to deter them, even affluence doesn't manage to corrupt them, because they are so directed towards their groups that the rest hardly counts. But what about their parents?

PARENTS WERE SHOCKED

If friends thought the convictions a joke, and employers didn't know or were amused, parents on the other hand were shocked and angry. (This was the overwhelming pattern for the whole sample.) The mother was generally more upset than the father. In the case of the grammar school boy, his parents were worried about his future career and kept the name out of the local papers. But for most other parents, after all, it was also their child's first appearance in court. By now they have mostly settled down to bitterness at the fine and the charge. Where the boys could not afford the fine or weren't given time to pay, the parents were the main people who paid up or helped to pay. One boy's parents are paying *him* back half the fine, though he has paid it into court himself: they think it so unfair. That is a bizarre exception, but it cast some light on the relation between these parents and their young. (The young are even sometimes exemplary: three-quarters of the Mods give over a third of their take-home pay to their parents, one gives half. Rockers give from a fifth to a quarter. Mids are midway.)

Rockers, in their self-sufficient way, hardly ever tell their parents about their worries. Their parents usually want to know what they're doing but rarely find out. They have bursts of complaining about their sons' behaviour; their sons are under no illusion that they behave as their parents would like, but they don't mind.

Mods usually tell parents about their worries, and they quite often tell what they are doing if they are asked. Parents rarely complain about their behaviour, though the Mods feel they only occasionally behave as their parents would like. But also they only occasionally care.

I wouldn't want boys at this age to kowtow to their parents. But it

is surprising, when so many lived at home, that so few parents had any
clue they were going to Margate last Whitsun. Parents have a long way
to go before they fill the gap the other institutions can't fill. But perhaps
it is the institutions that must move. Or is orientation towards the age
group here for good? America would imply so. But a survey of this
kind—perhaps fortunately—can't predict the future.

14

The Teenage Criminal
TERENCE MORRIS

11 APRIL 1963

By a curious stroke of irony the original draft of this article was lying on my desk overnight as a 16 year old burglar systematically rifled the drawers; whether in his purposeful scrutiny of the room and its contents he glanced at the title is a matter of conjecture. What is a matter of fact is that he is among the 10,000 boys between 14 and 17 who will be convicted of breaking and entering during 1963 in England and Wales. Of the 38,000 men and boys of all ages who are likely to be convicted of this crime, 70 per cent will be under the age of 21; about 25 per cent will be between the ages of 14 and 17 and around 20 per cent between 17 and 21. Clearly this lad will have ample company on his progress through the courts and the penal system but the question remains—how far is he typical of his generation?

So much attention has been concentrated on juvenile delinquency in particular and teenage misbehaviour in general that for what must be a sizeable proportion of the adult population the term teenager has become virtually synonymous with delinquent, sexually promiscuous, antisocial youth. The postwar period is littered with cast off pejorative epithets describing successive stages in the development of contemporary youth culture—spiv, cosh boy, Teddy boy, beatnik—each an imprecise, inaccurate or deliberately distorted term used in a wide variety of public contexts and often by those who ought to have known better. Even if he is not actually engaged in crime the "teenager" is often assumed to be a potential anarchist, particularly in the field of morals and politics, and the CND movement in its civil disobedience which has resulted in young people being arrested and imprisoned, has in one sense clinched the suspicion that the dividing line between crime and political radicalism is quite arbitrarily drawn. Disrespect for the institutions of property has come to be seen on the same contimium as contempt for empire, the independent nuclear deterrent, Macmillan and the royal family, to say nothing of the sexual norms implicit in *Scouting for Boys*.

Such muddled thinking is indicative of two inter-related phenomena: a conflict between adolescents and their elders, and social change. Surveys like Abrams' *Teen Age Consumer* have shown just how far adolescents have money in their pockets compared with their fathers a generation before; indeed, whole industries now sway to trends in the teenage market. Spending power, and a degree of economic independence, encourage an assertiveness that adults find disquieting. Adolescents are often resented both because they are assertive and because they are so much better off than youth before the war. To confound the situation still further, the class boundaries in adolescent culture that once existed in British society are fast disappearing.

Although Abrams speaks of the teenage market as characteristically working class, it is only so in that working class youngsters go to work sooner and have perhaps more money to spend. Grammar and public school boys also buy pop records, go to coffee bars, and ride motor scooters. And CND, to the dismay of so many middle class parents draws its recruits from an astonishingly wide social spectrum. Teenagers tend to look more and more alike, but it does not follow that they *are* alike. Contrary to what some of their elders believe, there are real differences in sociological terms between the housebreaker and the squatter in Trafalgar Square or the avid reader of *Private Eye*.

Although the teenage delinquent has become to be thought of as one of the special problems of our time, there is nothing essentially new here at all. Crime, as far as statistics can tell us, has been the preserve of youth since the beginning of the century. It is just that there are more adolescents and proportionately more adolescents being brought before the courts. But before discussing what is actually known about teenage crime we need to define "teenager". One literal definition is to include individuals who have passed their 13th birthdays but have not yet attained the age of 20. This raises several problems. For one thing it is an arbitrary age span; secondly it assumes a homogeneity

among the 13 to 19 age group which almost certainly does not exist
because of the wide social and emotional gulf which separates those
who are still in compulsory education and those who are earning
their own living. Thirdly, this definition fails to accommodate—or
even indicate—social class differentials in the behaviour of the age
group 13 to 19+. In contrast to many primitive societies we lack any
formal *rites de passage* whereby the change from dependent child to
independent adult is symbolized. In our own society a ceremonial act
around the age of puberty might well be impossible, if only because a
significant minority of young people continue in full time education
until they are 21 or 22. Our society is curiously ambivalent about what
young people in this age group may or may not do. Until his 21st
birthday everyone is an "infant" in the eyes of the law. However
"infants" may marry at 16 (with parental consent) although they must
wait a year longer before they may legally drive a motor car. At 18
boys used to be conscripted into the armed services and be required
to assist in the execution of political policies involving the use of force,
while having no say in the business of elections for a further 3 years.
And, once passed the 18th birthday an "infant" may also be lawfully
hanged.

STATISTICS ARE INADEQUATE

The years between 15 and 20 are, for many young people, years of
confusion in a period during which the process of maturation is possibly
at its maximum rate. Moreover these are the years in which the
business of social selection for occupational and educational opportunity is accomplished. They are also the years in which social class
differences in role assignment are at their greatest. Below 15 all children
are school children; beyond 21 or 22 all persons are regarded as adults.
In the years between, assigned roles range all the way from that of
schoolboy to that of husband and father.

The concept of the "teenager" is an artificial creation. It owes much
of its existence to the mass media in general and to pop culture in
particular, both of which have contributed towards the formation of a
stereotype. This stereotype is fundamentally lower class in that the
individual has left full time education at 15 and has entered full time
employment.

He has money in his pocket to spend, and he is sexually aware if not active, though possibly much less so than is commonly believed. The lyric writers in the pop field have in some ways created a role with which such young people can identify and so avoid certain of the disadvantages of the social limbo to which society has consigned them.

PERCENTAGES OF TOTAL CONVICTIONS APPLICABLE TO EACH AGE GROUP, 1961

Age	8-13	14-16	17-20	21-29	30+	Total
Larceny	18·3	16·5	16·0	20·6	28·6	100·0
Breaking and entering	27·3	24·9	18·6	19·7	9·5	100·0
Receiving	16·2	17·6	12·4	21·5	32·3	100·0
Fraud	2·2	3·2	8·7	28·2	57·7	100·0
Sex offences	4·3	14·9	17·7	22·2	40·9	100·0
Violence against the person	2·6	12·3	26·1	33·9	25·1	100·0
Robbery	11·2	13·5	29·1	35·8	10·4	100·0

What, precisely, do we know about the extent of crime and delinquency among teenagers? The answer is a little, but not nearly enough. There are really only two ways of finding out, either by carrying out a comprehensive national survey (which would cost an astronomical sum) or by combing the pages of the annual criminal statistics. The criminal statistics have three crucial limitations:

The problem of crime reporting. Only *indictable* (i.e. the most serious) offences are recorded as crimes known to the police. But a number of factors influence the degree to which indictable offences come to the notice of the police. There is often unwillingness to prosecute on the part of the victim, or the offence is considered to be relatively trivial. The result is the creation of the so-called iceberg effect, whereby a proportion of crime remains unknown to the police, and, perhaps more importantly whereby the ratio of known to unknown crime cannot be computed. *Non-indictable* offences are not recorded by the police in the same way; such offences are often of the kind that would not be reported by a third party—such as failing to take out a dog licence or travelling on the railway without having paid the proper fare. The bulk of non-indictable offences only become known when proceedings are being taken against an offender. The chances are that the submerged portion of them is very great.

Limitations imposed by the "clear-up rate". In 1961 only 44·8 per cent of the indictable offences known to the police were "cleared up"; that is to say an offender was detected or prosecuted. Thus in well over 50 per cent of all indictable offences there is no information about the offender. We know absolutely nothing about the offenders who get away. Hence the crime rates which are constructed from data on persons found guilty are prone to error in that those who get caught may not be representative of the offender population as a whole.

Age groupings. The statistics use standard age groupings which do not completely cover the period of adolescence. For while the age groups 14 and under 17 and 17 and under 21 cover the teenage period effectively, 13 year olds are lumped into the category "8 and under 14", and this group is not as homogeneous as the other two.

Bearing in mind that the information is not representative and the extent of its bias is unknown what *do* the Criminal Statistics tell us about teenage delinquency? The table below provides a profile of the persons found guilty of indictable offences in 1938 and in 1961.

CONVICTION FOR INDICTABLE CRIME PER 100,000 OF THE POPULATION, 1938 AND 1961

Males	8-13	14-16	17-20	21-29	30+	Total
1938	798	1,131	767	487	173	393
1961	1,425	2,535	2,275	1,377	300	818
Females						
1938	46	90	102	68	39	51
1961	142	310	265	152	72	111

It can be seen that male crime rates exceed female rates by a wide margin, notwithstanding increased rates for both sexes since 1938. The highest rates of conviction for all indictable crimes committed by both males and females also occur in the same age range 14-21. If, on the other hand, conviction rates are tabulated for each year of age one curious fact emerges, namely that the peak age for male convictions has consistently been in the last year of compulsory schooling—in 1938 13+ and in 1961 14+. Among females, however, the peak age has fallen from 19 in 1938 to 14+ in 1961.

Far and away the most frequent of all indictable offences known to the police are those against property—larceny and breaking and entering. Other important, but less common offences are those of receiving, frauds and false pretences, sexual offences and violence against the person. The table on p. 131 shows the percentage of the total of all convictions for those offences related to each age group. What this confirms is that taking the 14–17 and 17–21 age groups together, convictions for larceny, breaking and entering, violence against the person and robbery appear to be concentrated in the teenage sector of the population. But it is also clear that the young adults between 21 and 30 form by themselves a group in which convictions are also high. (It is interesting to compare with the fact that although illegitimate births appears to be unduly concentrated among teenage girls, bastard offspring are born to women between 21 and 30 with almost equal frequency when calculating illegitimate birth rates per *unmarried* woman at risk.) The pattern is not unlike that of 1938, save for the case of violence against the person in which the teenage share of convictions has more than doubled.

The problem of ascertaining the teenage contribution to non-indictable offences is more difficult because of the factors which may influence prosecutions. The table below shows the crude members of persons summarily convicted of non-indictable offences. Two types of offence stand out as being characteristic of the under 21 age group, taking and driving away motor cars, and malicious damage. Unfortunately, we do not know how far youthfulness is itself a factor in getting caught as well as a factor in the aetiology of delinquent behaviour, but even allowing for this it remains that delinquent behaviour is *comparatively* rare for it can be seen that in no age category does the conviction rate for indictable offences exceed 3 per cent of the total of all those at risk. Even if this figure were doubled—or even trebled—to offset the "iceberg effect" and the limitations of the "clear up" rate it would still mean that 90 per cent of youngsters in their teens do *not* commit delinquent acts.

COMPARISONS BY AGE AND SEX OF SUMMARY CONVICTIONS FOR SPECIFIC
OFFENCES, 1961

Males	8-13	14-16	17-20	21+	Total
Taking and driving away	329	3,757	4,894	3,409	12,389

Males	8-13	14-16	17-20	21+	Total
Malicious damage	3,924	3,042	3,319	4,381	14,666
Malicious injuries to property*	701	422	479	674	2,276

Females					
Taking and driving away	8	40	50	16	114
Malicious damage	87	68	51	512	457
Malicious injuries to property*	24	4	6	21	55

HIDDEN DELINQUENCY

Apart from unwillingness to prosecute young people, and the fact that families and schools deal with a good deal of deviant behaviour without recourse to the formal machinery of law enforcement, it might well be asked whether there are other forms of behaviour which occur beyond the limits of parental control. One of these areas is what might be broadly termed drug addiction. In this country addiction is not a serious problem; the Home Office estimate of addicts places the number under 500. (See Edwin Schur: *Narcotic Addiction in Britain and America*. 1962.) True addiction to opium derivatives is undoubtedly limited, but the extent to which other drugs are taken is as yet unknown. In the last decade the prescription of a wide variety of drugs in pill form for the treatment of mental disturbance has increased considerably and there is evidence that in London at least there exists the nucleus of a black market in those drugs which have a stimulant or euphoric effect.

Marihuana in the form of reefer cigarettes is also obtainable in the underworld of the metropolis. Reports of groups of young people indulging in the sniffing of ether or drycleaning fluid (carbon tetrachloride) are not uncommon, and in California attempts have been made to limit or prohibit the sale of the balsa cement used in model making, since it was discovered that adolescents were sniffing it in order to obtain a euphoric effect.

This is an area in which accurate information is acutely lacking, though there is reason to suspect that it is limited to metropolitan

* Indictable offences dealt with summarily.

centres and occurs among young people who have left home and are to some extent living relatively disorganized lives on the fringe of the urban underworld. To what extent teenagers who use drugs are also involved in crime is far from clear. John Terry, executed for the capital murder of a bank guard in Worthing in 1961, claimed to have regularly chewed "purple hearts", the name given to a particular form of benzedrine and dexedrine, and also to have been "possessed" by the spirit of the long deceased New York hoodlum Legs Diamond.

The trial court placed little credence in these claims and treated Terry as if he were a completely normal person. By and large drug use is indicative of a retreatist rather than assertive social pattern, and it is unlikely therefore to be widespread among active delinquents.

The information available about teenage delinquency, then, is both limited and variable in character. Firstly there is a real possibility that those concerned with the machinery of justice may see the problem as bigger than it really is if only because of the marked increase in the numbers of young people actually passing through the courts. The whole system of law enforcement and penal practice is so balanced that even a small increase in the teenage crime rate could produce serious effects on the operation of the system. Secondly, a point often overlooked, the contribution to crime made by young adult males between 21 and 30 is considerable, and in respect of some offences such as robbery and violence against the person the rate of convictions is very similar to that found among the teenage group. Teenagers are not the only serious offenders. On the other hand where violence against the person is concerned there has been a remarkable shift in the age structure of those convicted since 1938. While for juveniles under 14 the increase in the proportion of all convictions has only increased from 2·3 per cent, to 2·6 per cent, the 14–17 group which accounted for only 5 per cent of all convictions in 1938 now has 12·3 per cent; and the 17–21 group which formerly had only 10·3 per cent of all convictions now has 26·1 per cent of the total. With the exception, then, of violence against the person and of robbery, the age distribution of the proportions of the total found guilty of the commonest indictable offences remains much as it was before the war.

Thirdly, it is true that while many young offenders are "normal" in the sense that they do not display gross mental abnormality or the symptoms of mental illness, there is another sense in which the delinquent is not a normal teenager. He tends to come from an urban slum background in which the stimuli for and approval of law breaking are considerable, and these neighbourhoods are in a minority, even in big cities. Although J. B. Mays has argued (in *Growing up in the City*) that in certain areas delinquent behaviour is a standardized part of growing up it is still "abnormal" when viewed against the general picture. To put it another way, because delinquency is normal in a Liverpool slum it does not follow that it is normal everywhere, if only because Liverpool type slums are themselves a comparative rarity in the national picture.

The fact that delinquents in this sense are atypical tends to be masked by their participation with non-delinquents in a common youth culture—a world of pop songs, scooters, coffee bars, juke boxes, and elegant if somewhat *avant garde* styles of dress. The result is that many adults assume that certain aspects of this youth culture are synonymous with a commitment to delinquency, which is a long way from the truth. To get at the truth is an exacting task, and one in which we have made little headway so far.

15

The Long Blunt Shock

NEALE PHAROAH

26 SEPTEMBER 1963

"You are sentenced to three months detention"

Those seven words marked, finally and irrevocably, my last glimpse of the outside world for 3 months; on Monday, 10th December at 9 o'clock, I walked to the courtroom expecting a heavy fine, and at 10 o'clock, after several minutes standing before two magistrates, the Press, and the public, sentence was passed. Shaken, amazed and a little frightened, I was led down from the dock by two policemen to a tiny cell beneath the courts, and when their car had arrived I was taken back to the police station. Within 2 hours I had made desperate attempts to tell my parents, arrange care of my flat and my belongings, and was speeding on my way to the particular centre the magistrates had chosen.

It was only later that I realized how fortunate I was in such rapid transit; my arrest occurred on a Thursday, bail was permitted until Monday and on Tuesday my sentence had begun; most of the detainees I met at the centre had waited for anything between 1 and 10 weeks on remand or awaiting sentence prior to reception at their actual place of detention, which seemed a trifle unjust, since people who completed a three month sentence had, in fact, served an appreciably longer time. However, the car was nearing its destination. We travelled for what must have been 3 miles after turning off the main road, passing alternately through dense woods and bare stretches of flat desolate land.

The last house was passed some way back, and a cold blue noticeboard announced arrival. The surrounding countryside was as remote to me as the high barbed wire fence that enclosed the institution. Through the heavy iron gates, up a drive, through an oaken door and yet another barrier and I was inside the main block having already seen the first few faces of my fellow inmates.

Reception procedure was simple, giving an insight into what lay ahead and beginning the minor hardships and trivial degradations which then looked so overwhelming. As in entering the forces, it started with signing forms and ended with the shortest haircut you are ever likely to have in your life. The necessary forms signed, my pockets emptied, I was stripped and given a set of kit standard in most institutions, consisting of a blue tunic, striped shirt, blue tie, grey flannel trousers and cumbersome black shoes; after a bath I donned the unfamiliar clothing and was a prisoner. The officer doing reception duty was large and stern, but not unpleasant, and quickly gave my first lesson in detention centre life: all officers, the uniformed members of the prison service, were to be called sir; one said either *yes, sir* or *no, sir* to them and nothing else, and respect was to be shown to them at all times; the primary virtue I was to concern myself with was obedience whether the command was distasteful, ridiculous or even wrong. It was to obey at all times, without question and in all places. I was handed a leaflet that the governor had had printed to prepare new inmates for what was required of them.

> You have been sent here by the courts for a short course in moral, social and physical discipline.

He reminded me that:

> Manners maketh man

and that I could gain one-sixth remission of my sentence for good behaviour and lose it very easily; that I could write one letter per week, receive one letter per week, that I could appeal and that finally I could see the governor from Monday to Friday on matters of "inside" or "outside" importance. After spending a short time in the cells known later in their truer function as "punishment cells" I was marched by the officer, with a smiling but alien inmate, clutching my pillow-case filled with shaving kit, toothbrush, soap and washing materials under one arm and boots, overalls and gaiters under the other, to my cell in A wing, a long block of single cells occupied by inmates in the first stages of their sentences. It was half past four in the afternoon. I was a prisoner. I had committed a crime and was paying for it. I had stolen: I was losing my freedom.

The impressions that followed are still very vivid; only now are they beginning to recede.

That afternoon, just before the evening meal, I made my first contact with the boys—whom I saw standing at ease at the doors of their cells as I was, waiting for the order to march off to the dining hall along the corridor after washing and changing from overalls. As soon as I was seen, I was plied with questions about the outside world. Just as rapidly I asked them about what I was now facing. They asked me the latest record at the top of the popularity charts and I replied with the question that preoccupied me more than the prison routine itself: how fast did time pass there? It was little consolation to be told that it went astonishingly fast. Because it was comparatively minor, my offence was of paramount interest, news of it passing from cell to cell till it was known to all; we came to recognize each other by our various crimes—not so various, though, as one might imagine. The greater proportion of the inmates as far as I could gather, were "in" either for motoring charges or house and shop breaking, both quick-reward crimes which require little thought and often occur as a direct result of similar pressures; those of status value, in a young environment, of the motor car or cycle. I received much evidence for this conclusion from their continual arguments on the merits of specific makes and types of vehicle, and of the money needed to fulfil the symbols of our adolescent values, obtained by simple theft. The other offences consisted of assault, usually on a policeman previously singled out as a recognized opponent to their activities in the area, or, more often, any unfortunate who was "in the way" after a dance or drinking session. One met the single cases where detention was given for breaking probation or just *suspicion* of a multiple number of crimes, again usually petty theft, and one heard of others punished for more individual transgressions, but they represented a very small proportion of the total. What surprised me most was the vast difference in intelligence and practical ability of my fellows in contrast to their background and social responsibilities.

Most—like me—had seen family stress in the near or distant past and had failed to form a satisfactory relationship with one or both parents. All had tended to build an environment which was conducive to short-term decisions and to "chance" living from day to day without much thought of longer than a week ahead; this had developed in some to such an extent that the prospect of a prison sentence was viewed very much as an occupational hazard and a matter of luck. This attitude varied between the rather large fraction who would undoubtedly repeat their crimes, in their own and officers opinions, and those who would never offend again; but quite definitely the attitudes existed. I even found it in myself, believing it bad luck in getting what was perhaps a heavier punishment than I was prepared for, in fact in getting caught at all.

Background and attitude, offence and outlook, appeared at that stage to be very similar. Admittedly this was after a relatively short contact with the 20 odd boys who were housed in the same wing as I, but my cursory opinion of one-third of the boys whom I came to know was justified towards the end of my detention when I had met far more and had made several friendships which have continued since my release (any free contact between us was quite naturally limited owing to the rigorous and closely supervised regimentation). This pattern of behaviour subsisted without regard for social class or basic intelligence; during my stay I met 70 boys, no less than four of whom had been to a grammar school, one to a private secondary school, and one to a commercial art school and who was reasonably competent despite having completed only half of his course. Including myself, this meant that 10 per cent were of above average intelligence, yet they had responded in precisely the same way to society as their counterparts with less powers of communication.

On the other end of the scale I met boys who had been in and out of approved schools, exhausted all the possibilities of probation and would almost certainly be graduated to a Borstal or prison; there was one who was virtually unable to read or write, not because he was incapable, but because he had just not bothered and there were those whose fathers had been in prison before them and had brothers, uncles and friends currently doing time. We were all in a detention centre.

It was, of course, a slow process to make enough acquaintance with my fellows to form any knowledge of their background and outlook, to build a coherent comparison with myself and to construct a conclusive picture of apparent similarities. It took the greater part of the 3 months I was here before I had the opportunity to speak to a sufficiently broad cross-section of detainees. The first week was spent in trying to adapt to the rigorous discipline and deprivations which I had to learn to accept until my release and in adjusting my body to prison food, strenuous physical training and work, which were exhausting me then. We marched, we ran, we scrubbed, we polished; I was shouted at, drilled, inspected and drilled again; there were medicals and fitness tests, sermons and an "education test"; until my first week had passed and the definite shock had changed to routine. I was not able to think of anything but the mixture of self-pity, helplessness and anger which so many of us felt at being forced into such intensely regulated, enclosed and uncomfortably familiar behaviour.

The centre itself was new and clean, it had been open for less than a year. It was approached by a straight concrete drive, bordered on one side by a playing field and a line of prefabricated houses belonging to the officers on the other. It led up to the main gate which was set in the wire fence surrounding the inner buildings. In the middle of the compound was a parade square around which the central block, the hospital, administration offices and gymnasium were arranged. The central block (with three extended wings, one of cells and two of dormitories) had one floor and was built in separate interconnecting units off a corridor running along the entrance to each wing, so that the building was shaped like a letter E.

On the opposite side of this corridor was the dining hall, with small tables seating four, followed by a modern, well-equipped kitchen which produced adequate, and substantial, if plain, food; further along there was a washroom with enough space for at least half of the entire centre to wash in, a row of toilets, a shower and bathroom, a laundry, a cloakroom and finally, a small washroom and a row of cells intended as a punishment block for persistent transgressors of discipline. Adjoining these was the reception office. Each one of these units was scrubbed out and if necessary, polished, each day—very often they were scrubbed more than once. Each wing was swept and kept clean and its single toilet washed. The corridor was treated in the same way. This scrupulous cleanliness was applied to our personal kit, to our lockers and equipment, and to ourselves.

Since my experience of any type of prison or institution is confined to this one it would be rash to make more than a tentative assertion that it was among the cleanest and best designed. However, as it has been in operation for rather less than a year and there is a great deal of accessible material on conditions in the other types of penal institutions, Borstals, reform schools and remand centres it would appear to be a reasonable claim. The officers at this centre had worked in most of the prisons in Great Britain and several of the Borstals and it was readily agreed that we were living in the best conditions available for this type of institution and were eating extremely good food. I cannot disagree.

A detention centre is designed to give offenders under the age of 21 a "short sharp shock" involving "a short course in moral, social and physical discipline" acting as a deterrent to further offences. Therefore the routine is of necessity unpleasant, stringently adhered to and enforced by the officers. Under the conditions they are subjected to feeling among the detainees runs high, and tempers run short, and it often happened that this could only be dissipated by developing a real hatred for some of the stricter officers, with firm intentions of coming back after discharge and "doing him over", or by fighting each other— a breach of discipline which resulted in a loss of remission. Routine at the detention centre is such that the detainee is kept occupied and closely supervised throughout the day. Each day except Sunday was started with 15 minutes' PT on the parade ground at 6.30 a.m. followed by a wash, shave and breakfast. At 8.0 a.m. after a change into overalls and cleaning of the cells and dormitories there was a parade taken either by the governor or his principal officer. Then every boy in the institution was marched to the job allocated him for the labour period —which was from just after 8.0 a.m. until 4.30 p.m. with an hour for lunch and 2 short breaks at 10 and 3. From Monday to Friday each work party was subjected to 1 hour of PT in the gymnasium under the eye of a hard, burly PTI; in the course of a week we sweated our way through timed circuits; weight training, exercises, "punishment PT", gymnastics and basketball. There is much to be said for and against the type of training to which we had to adapt in the gymnasium, for while it is not unfounded to criticize an officer who forces his victims to hang from wallbars, run around with medicine balls above their heads, jump, bend, stretch, and do innumerable repetitive actions like press-ups to the point of real collapse it is fair to add that most boys gained in strength, weight and fitness in the process. Often the juncture is passed when the activity becomes a punishment and ceases to be beneficial, but one must bear in mind the intentions behind sending someone to a detention centre. These may or may not be wrong but must be complied with to test the efficacy of the intentions before one says that the PT there is over-emphasized. We all suffered "punishment" and "circuits"; we were all punched and driven to what we thought were our limits but we all played basketball and football, parading our newly discovered muscles in the knowledge that none of us felt any lasting ill-effects. At the close of the labour period and our daily PT there was a final parade involving a search for cigarettes, iron bars and ropes in case any detainee contemplated smoking or escaping. At 4.30 p.m. we marched in, cold and tired, were given five minutes to wash and change and taken to the dining room for a cooked tea. The period following tea was split up into one hour of reading our library books, which were changed weekly, and a further two hours at classes of pottery, motor mechanics, English, basic mathematics, general science or PT of a less strenuous nature. Each class did one or two subjects each night except Wednesday, when kit was changed and we were paid the meagre 1s 6d we earned that week in sweets. Unfortunately these classes were largely ineffective since they gave the only available opportunity of the day to relax while not under direct supervision of an officer; the word "education" tended to be purely nominal. If any detainee had transgressed one of the hundreds of minor regulations during the day, an extremely easy thing to do, the two pleasures of reading and classes were denied him and he spent what little energy he had left in polishing the corridors or washing up until it was time, at 8.30 p.m. for a mug of cocoa and bed. If the infringement warranted it, the extra work was extended until the weekend which was otherwise spent in reading, writing the single letter allowed each person, and preparing for a full Sunday inspection of all our kit laid out army style on our beds.

Any serious breach of discipline was rewarded with loss of remission or solitary confinement on a restricted diet, a beating, and in severe cases, a visiting magistrate, who could have prolonged the sentence or sent the offender to Borstal training. In the three months I was there I saw all except the latter inflicted for transgressions ranging from smoking, talking out of place, and losing kit, to having dirty boots on parade; nevertheless, the favourite treatment was work. Nothing but futile, senseless work fills our miserable recollections.

On the principle that detention is a brief period of hardship acting purely as a deterrent, it follows that the work is far from being constructive and is invariably destructive. During the early part of his sentence, the detainee is employed in the main block scrubbing floors and polishing them, not so much with the object of getting floors clean, since they already are, but simply to degrade the boy, otherwise no officer would have said:

> On your knees, boy, when you scrub here you do it with both hands on the brush and both knees firmly on the ground.

or on catching someone glancing at a scrap of newspaper salvaged from the offices, have shouted:

> You aren't here to read or think, boy, you are here to work.

at the same time twisting the unfortunate's ear and pushing him down to do the inevitable press-ups. When it was felt the detainees had learned from this they joined the other parties working in the fields, the kitchen, laundry and workshops up to the final weeks when they were trusted to work outside the compound, clearing and sweeping the roads then covered with snow and ice. In the kitchen, laundry, workshops and in cleaning the main block, the work is not hard though it may occasionally be ridiculous. Digging fields, clearing roads, and stripping lengths of telephone cable to sell the lead and copper inside is arduous especially in the weather condition that England had last winter. The ridicule and degradation grew to painful proportions when, clad in thin denim overalls and boots, with an overcoated and gloved officer complaining of the bitter cold, one was forced to move snow in temperatures below freezing with sore, numb, bleeding hands trying to grip one's shovel. It would not be difficult to imagine this sort of discipline effective in deterring anyone against committing crimes. But is it? Is it true to say that three months of blind obedience in digging holes, endless PT and continual unreasoning deprivation provides the emotive suggestion needed to serve as a deterrent when once more the offender is returned to his environment? And when that environment was largely responsible in providing the condition of mind which resulted in the offence leading to the detention and is likely to remain a catalyst to further deviation?

In an account of this nature it is not easy for the observer who is in full participation to retain that degree of objectivity needed for valid criticism; on one level there are all the frustrated emotions born of imprisonment and on the other level, relying on a limited personal interpretation, it is possible to reach a spurious conclusion, for the temptation exists to consider what previous observers have said, and in using their terminology to justify their conclusions with further examples in trite attempts to be socially conscious. It is probable that my experience could be tinged too strongly with emotion and there may be some discrepancy between what I felt, torn as I was in angry bitterness and acceptance of the mechanism of social punishment and what was felt by the rest of the detainees. In discussing, among my fellows, the reactions to the experiences to which we were subjected, I found they were very similar to my own.

All of them realized that they had done active wrong more than once and that some form of punishment should be levelled at them, but in many, this was a matter of chance and an unfortunate occurrence, leaving them with the reasoning that if there was a chance of getting caught, as there obviously was, the next time they "did a job" it would carry gain enough to outweigh the punishment.

After this, I ain't gonna do another job for a while, but when I do . . .

I also met a few who could firmly state that this had taught them a lesson. Punishment was accepted by all the people I met there, but it was felt that much of what we were subjected to was unnecessarily ridiculous, and that several officers enjoyed inflicting it.

There was no real contact between the officers and the detainees; for that was because their function in a detention centre was to supervise a formal routine, rather than direct those who could be directed, in the relatively short time they were in the centre. They appeared to fall into two types, the majority merely doing their job, remaining disinterested and maintaining some friendliness, and the minority allowing personal feelings and what seemed to me to be childish spite to govern their decisions. It was, I think, inevitable that this would happen on occasions but I did see and feel the incredible hatred that can arise in a reasonably calm boy for the officers who made it their duty to be permanently unpleasant.

I do know what it is like to work all day in freezing weather, come in to a warm building with five minutes to wash the first layer of grime off, change, and march into a dining hall and, after grabbing the nearest tray of food, be given extra work for not remembering to thank the officer standing by the kitchen hotplate (he had nothing to do with the food, he was just there to be thanked).

Many of the complaints I heard were common throughout the centre. The prominent one concerned the lack of medical attention given to the continual colds, coughs, influenza, and the more common sores and cuts which never healed. One unlucky fellow had an enormous swelling distending his cheek and reported sick to the medical officer who scrutinized him carefully and asked:

What's wrong with you!

The boy pointed to his cheek.

Well, what is it, come on I haven't got all day, you should know what the bloody thing is, you've got it, not me.

The boy got a mouthwash and two aspirins. Aspirin was the standard remedy for most complaints, even a sprained elbow.

One can easily recall a vast number of incidents which serve to indicate the heights to which the sense of ludicrousness and unwarranted "disciplining" can rise. Now I have forgotten what it was like to shave with a 10-day-old razor blade in 2 minutes, and to frantically polish kit and fold it into utmost geometric regularity for the governor's inspections or in preparation for the "grade" which one had to make on recommendation of five different officers concerned with work, cleanliness or PT and "attitude before discharge". I cannot remember the cold or the endless marching, neither am I able to recall the depressed moods in which most of my early letters were written; it is difficult to believe them when I read them now. I have been free for two weeks now.

Three months detention was a shock. However, all of us began to adapt very quickly to this, and it was no time at all before the shock became routine frustration. Any treatment of this kind is moderately successful in breaking habits and behaviour, but in replacing the offender in his environment, with no change in him or that environment, it seems to defeat what would be the real object (if old patterns are allowed to coalesce in the same way, as they will). The function of after-care is to rebuild behaviour; there is an after-care service following Borstal and prison, but the attitude adopted in detention centre policy seems to dispense with this in the hope that the "shock" will act as an effective deterrent. If the system is to continue in its present state, then after-care would be the logical way to increase the "success rate" (if one can agree with the somewhat arbitrary term as meaning no further offences committed). One is not taught at a detention centre, one cannot learn how to change in order to avoid going there again, except in experiencing the limits to which one's value structure can transgress that of established authority: value structure itself is not radically changed by this.

All that we discerned was the power behind the law and the prospect ahead of offending again, which is not a strong lesson to teach boys with the records and outlooks I noticed. We adapted rapidly to the centre despite its hardships; I discovered on discharge that I immediately readjusted to outside life as if I had never left it. If this happens with everybody, and I think it does, I do not see how the treatment can be fully effective against those for whom it was designed. Moreover I got the impression that everybody I saw there, wearing the same clothes and living in the same conditions as I was, did not need to spend half his life in a prison, and this feeling of wasted ability applied just as much to the young men who were labelled "recidivist" as to the intelligent ones who may easily change, given the right stimulus. It appeared to me that most of them had trouble channelling their ability into a satisfactory occupation.

My offence was theft of spirits from my employers just before Christmas; perhaps the way to test my progression is to work there again next year at the same time. . . .

16

Beat and Gangs on Merseyside

COLIN FLETCHER

20 FEBRUARY 1964

Out of the unemployment, the endless two-up-and-two-downs with tin baths in the cobbled yards, among the smell of oil, salt and cattle-cake, has come an adolescent phenomenon that culminated last week in the successful export of the Mersey product to the US. Between the age of 14 and 18 I was a member of two Merseyside gangs. At the age of 16 I became the singer and bass-guitarist of a "rock group". How the beat invaded the gangs and changed them beyond all recognition is one of the little known aspects of the Mersey story.

Gangs in Liverpool and Birkenhead took the same pattern as the adult association of men: a strict geographical delineation. Gangs developed with the same notion of territory as held by the men who gathered at the local every evening, but with an acceptable alternative to the pub: the chippy on the turf—a chip shop in the gang's area—or possibly a coffee bar.

The chippy was the centre of all action in the winter for the Holly Road gang—my first and urban gang. It was always warm with a favourite smell and a Pepsi-Cola would legitimize a good half-evening. Parents and other adults used to scuttle in and out but being friends of the owner we were allowed to stay. The owner was very important to us as in return for a night's "protection" he would issue the evening's left-overs free of charge.

The chippy for the Park Gang—my second—was the climax of the evening. At 9 p.m. a long straggling line of boys and girls made their way up the hill. The fish cakes were ready and the bottles of orangeade waited. To a gang a chip shop was an essential prerequisite and a place to go regularly even after being out all evening. Looking back, I see now that what brought us into the gang and into the chippy every night was our feelings of insecurity. The epithet "teenager" implies that one has arrived at some stage in evolution but everything inside is jangling and jerking.

School, too, played its part in gang formation. At school we found out who lived near and who didn't. We discovered the different types of boys who made up the area. Most important of all we found the most reliable, tough and fair boy who was to become the gang's leader.

The Holly Road Gang was relatively small, though it was typical of those in an older working class urban area. Partly because of its size it acted as a buffer state between two stronger gangs who always thought that physical violence was the only way to solve their differences in opinion over which was the better gang. Holly Road had its fighters and thieves, its lovers and artists. In the Park Gang, which I knew better, it was the same.

As defence and warfare were high upon any gang's list of actions the "belligerents" were always considered important. These boys often fell into two categories; those who always wanted to fight and those who were always good at it. In every gang known there was a hard core. It was normally two brothers or "life-long" friends. In the Holly Road Gang there were the O'Haras and in the Park Gang were Bresso and Ronnie. These were the boys who could go in first and come out best. They had a social rank almost as high as that of the gang leader because, like him, they could go anywhere, across anybody's turf, and not be challenged.

When one of these boys left the Park Gang, Jack, our leader, said "I always felt safe with you". This was the biggest compliment that could be paid by a leader to a member because Jack, by nature of his job, had to be able to at least hold his own with any one person. Barnies or punch-ups were common but regulated. We fought for our status, not for fun. A fight was the result of consultations between the leader and his lieutenants; except when under attack. The Ferry Boys or the Tombstones (who were based at cemetery gates) had to disturb the balance of gangs or beat up a member or swipe one of the gang's girls before action came and then it was a concerted night's work.

Disturbance of the balance of gangs was infrequent. One such time was when the Ferry Boys laid into the Broadways and smashed their hut as well as everybody they found in it. This occurrence obviously worried every gang in the area. The Ferries would become too brash and rough with every gang and its property if they were allowed to continue. The leader of the Tombstones came to see Jack and they met on the neutral territory of a border street corner. Both gangs were about 10 yards behind just in case. The two leaders agreed that the Ferries could only be beaten badly by a combined force. Two members were sent to bring the remnants of the Broadways and we made our way by four separate routes down towards the station and the Ferry. We didn't thrash the Ferries on any principle of justice, but to reassert the positions of gangs in the neighbourhood.

Two Kinds of Crime

The "criminals" were either gang-based or gang-supported. They were gang-based when the idea, which was their own, involved a great deal of risk, or the penalty if caught was likely to be severe. The gang-supported crimes were those annual—almost traditional—affairs to which the majority of the police force closed their eyes (cycle races through the park, letting ourselves in and out of the park-keeper's shed to make a cup of tea, and scrumping in orchards and gardens). Vandalism was not the aim of the exercise but there must have been some damage.

The most popular gang-based activity was prizing cigarette machines off the wall to obtain the money and weeds. It was not uncommon, also, for the local sweets and tobacconists to "get done" regularly. Many of the boys worked on newspaper rounds which gave them an intimate knowledge of the shop.

The police, however, were very well aware of the paper-round/ breaking and entering relationship and a small number of arrests were almost guaranteed. Most leaders, too, were against serious crimes as the gang was then constantly under the strain of fear of arrest. The Holly Road Gang, because it had less fighting potential, turned very gradually to crime as its main interest. The leader was not a "criminal" and did his best to hold the gang together. Disappointed with his performance a large section of the criminal element left the gang and these boys then adopted a leader who had the glamour of "inside" experience. He led these boys through a long series of cunning petty felonies, getting more bold and less careful until various "stretches" split this little gang completely. The Holly Road Gang continued in a very much modified form which allowed new influences to have a greater effect.

Jack, of the Park Gang, was equally effective a regulator of crime as he was of warfare. He removed the criminal element's support by placing them very slightly out of the intimacy of the gang whenever they had a foolhardy scheme. The "criminals" were told to go and natter behind the shed if they couldn't talk about anything else. Many potential knock-offs were also averted by his refusal to allow "hot stuff" to be dumped in the gang's cellar. Jack looked after the gang by adhering to social standards when their contravention might have been detrimental.

The "romantics" helped themselves and the gang at the same time. They were the "good-lookers" who brought the birds to the gang by going out with them first and then, when the girl went out with another member they took to the sea of troubles again. They were seldom fighters and spent most of their time, as one "criminal" remarked, "standing in the chippy half looking at themselves in the mirror". Fred was a persistent romantic. Nobody knew how he succeeded but he always managed to find a girl from another territory and then just happen to be out with yet another when the girl's gang arrived to settle ownership!

Set apart from the gang was the "spiritual" element. Even if there was more than one person in it, it was still very small, though it could be very powerful. The "spiritual" boys could constrain the gang in the leader's absence. Its main functions were counselling for the members and advice for the leader. As the Park Gang was large it had two such members, who were both older and practising Christians. They were in constant demand in times of "rozzer rash" (when the gang was severely nettled by the police) and they kept the gang ticking over by just listening to troubles and advising the leader as to which members were directly responsible and who were the gullible youths.

The "musical" type was latent. In the Park Gang there was the boy who played a good harmonica; the one who was adept at a rhythm with knitting needles on a lamp post; the singer who never smiled and two harmonizers who picked up tunes readily but could never remember the words. There was a similar motley talent in the Holly Road Gang but they shouted more and took entertaining the gang far less seriously.

The leader of a gang needed to fit in with the unique arrangement of these elements within it. The Tombstones had a large belligerent section and so their leader was picked primarily for his physical prowess. The Park Gang had an equilibrium of types and Jack was chosen by the respect he had from each element, combined with the ability to control.

Pride in one's gang was high. Members always lived in the reflection of the group as a whole. If we had been beaten up then we felt rotten and listless. We all grumbled and blamed ourselves for a poor attempt. We believed we lost because we were not on form, rather than because the other gang had better fighters. We were all responsible for the gang's name.

Members looked upon the girls in the gang with an ambivalent attitude. For most of the time girls were supposed to be secondary; a mere accessory for living one's life in the gang. Sexual experience was of real importance only to the "romantics". A girl belonged to a gang because she lived on the turf. She did not have to join the gang, though most did, but it was ill-advised to join another. A girl was a drag if around too often or with the same boy too long. This idea of a girl being the property of the whole gang had great expression on gang outings. Every gang went every night possible to a visiting fun fair. The fair itself was considered neutral territory so the visit became a non-violent expression of talent. Girls fitted the bill. Their laughter and screams on the waltzers and dodge'ms, their appreciation of the gifts of bric-à-brac won by performing some feat and their physical attractiveness were all "notches on the gang's belt". Pride in the gang's girls and fighting record were central in its life.

The gang, between the periods 1954 and 1958, was not only a microcosm of society; it was relatively speaking the only society the adolescent knew and felt sure of. This was the situation when rock and roll arrived on Merseyside.

ANIMAL RHYTHM

The arrival of rock and roll (words now consigned to the adolescent's scrap heap) in Merseyside was preceded by rumour. Almost every local picture house banned Bill Haley and his Comets, but there had been rumour that *Rock Around the Clock* had more effect on teenagers all over the world than any other film. The Bill Haley riots for the Holly Road Gang were on a traditional Saturday night in 1955. The queue outside the Palais was large but quite orderly. There were many gangs present, but the pact of neutral territory held good.

Gangs filed in and filled up row after row. Unlike most of the films, this one had commanded an almost entirely adolescent audience. When the music started it was infectious—no one managed to keep still. It was the first time the gang had been exposed to an animal rhythm that matched their behaviour. Soon couples were in the aisles copying the jiving on the screen. The "bouncers" ran down to stop them. The audience went mad. Chairs were pulled backwards and forwards, arm rests uprooted, in an unprecedented orgy of vandalism. There were fourteen seats missing when it was "Queenie" time.

But the sound, new and exciting as it was, took some time to catch on. It was regarded as part of America. For the local adolescents and their gangs it was a little too polished, especially with that brass line-up, to be imitated.

Then the beat spread like a rumour; the interpretations were more important than the original. Saturday night had always been the climax of the week when boots were exchanged for polished shoes and a truce was called to allow free movement across town and city. The Saturday night meeting time had always been 7 o'clock but it was suddenly changed to 7.30 p.m. This radical move was caused by BBC's new contribution to the passing craze, "6-5 Special".

This show was very important, because it was more amateurish, as were all British attempts at the time, and this made copying very much easier. There were more "numbers" to choose from and the guitar started wholly to replace trumpets and saxophones. Elvis Presley's "Heartbreak Hotel" realized the potential of a barrage of guitars. Slightly later Buddy Holly and the Crickets made the point eminently clear with their first record "That'll be the Day". Ten members of the Park Gang bought this record—starting a habit that they were unlikely to give up—and the musical element found the hammering thrown-out beat easy and most enjoyable to imitate. Guitars and a set of drums were needed to succeed in a reasonable rendering but this idea was only a suggestion for four months.

All the local gangs fitted this new phenomenon into their lives with curiosity and interest. On going down to Holly Street I found that this gang had a much more advanced interpretation of the music. They were interested in the movement rather than the expression of beat. They preferred the numbers with "bags of body" in them. The more solid the noise the more they liked it.

For the next six months an increasing amount of the gang's time was taken up with listening to pop records. It was winter and the Park shed inevitably lost most of its attraction; the regular attendance of 50 members was decimated. Groups of friends broke away and were necessarily small as a record player could normally function only in someone's front room—the back room housed the rival telly. Members' attitudes towards listening to records varied greatly. The romantics obviously found the habit a good way of getting together and their parties became based upon jiving to the latest releases. Some of the "criminals" and "belligerents" found the new outlet a little hard to accept: it was "soft". For them there seemed to be nothing immediate, no virility-cum-violence in the records.

When the spring came and, without a signal, the Park Gang gradually reassembled, the beat and what should be done about it was foremost in our minds and conversation. This preoccupation with the new sound was usurping some of the old habits. There was no apparent decrease in violence but there was a great actual decrease in the desire to "rumble". The music, like the roughness, was gradually becoming "us". An additional attraction, especially as we were getting older, was the effect of the music on girls. They seemed to be "real gone"— another recently rejected term—over not only the sound but also those who made it. All these ideas slowly led to the formation of the gang's own group.

All over Merseyside gangs were giving birth to groups. Each gang had its musical element who had naturally become interested and then involved in the sound of rock. This natural affinity was encouraged by gangs and the musical boys needed little encouragement. They had been stuck with 1930's ballads too long to miss their chance. The group inevitably came from the gang as there were very few boys on Merseyside strong enough to resist joining one.

The Holly Road Gang had managed to acquire the help of a friendly woodwork master. This man gave them the active encouragment to "get off pipe-racks and on to something they could use" (his words). As there were a number of gangs in that school the woodwork shop developed into a little factory for guitar-making.

ROCK ON THE GRASS

In June 1958, following the trend, the Park Gang gave birth to the "Tremoloes". There had been excited anticipation when four of the musical element started to learn to play the guitar. The gang had no real notion of what a rock group looked like until these boys came down to the shed with their instruments one night and played for half an hour. The gang jived on the grass and clapped wildly after every item.

At this time I joined the group as singer and bass-guitarist. Soon the group began to practise regularly and some of the gang members pooled their knowledge and made two large amplifiers. The combination of terrific noise and regular practising soon made it impossible to practise in a front room. The gang scoured the turf for deserted houses, bomb shelters and finally church halls. Many church halls and youth clubs were glad to get the lads in somehow and the youth leaders were quite amazed at the number of people the group brought along.

Soon it became a regular thing for the gang actively to support every practice. The group was becoming the gang's totem. The gang had started to rival other gangs on a totally new level. As the process of producing a group from within a gang's ranks was cumulative one could feel the decline of tension in other forms of competition. What mattered now was not how many boys a gang could muster for a Friday night fight but how well their group played on Saturday night. By autumn there had been an almost total shift of interest.

The Park Gang literally nursed its group. To enable the group to buy microphones and speakers a system of "shares" was set up which were to be repaid from the group's earnings. Any member of the gang could buy any number of shares and in this way help the group to compete successfully with the groups of rival gangs. The trusted "spiritual" boys became the director and manager respectively. An electrical apprentice acted as an on-the-spot repairer when the amplifiers or guitar pick-ups failed.

Funds provided a battered old van and with three borrowed cars the group and its fans toured the dance halls. The fee paid to the group was taken to cover the cost of dance tickets. This wealth of support had two major effects on the group. Our fans gave us a great deal of confidence: whatever we did, whatever its quality, they were enthusiastic. The gang enabled the group to be spontaneous, natural and free in its interpretations. Second, although the traditional peace pact for Saturday night travellers was still in operation it was a different matter when two rival groups arrived at the same hall for the same booking. This kind of thing happened frequently when the system of dances first started and it was then a case of battle royal. The gang fought for its group while the players protected their instruments and amplifiers.

EVOLUTION OF THE GANG

Girls, too, assumed a new role. They became seamstresses. The group needed uniforms and yet could not afford the £100 for a set of four beat outfits. These beginnings of idiomatic clothing were within the group though soon the gang identified itself with the group by copying the group's clothes. The Tombstone's group wore black suits and white ties and the gang followed this style very quickly.

By the spring of 1959 the two gangs described were unrecognizable in the terms used. The breakaway of the criminals from the Holly Road Gang was rapidly followed by the breakaway of the same type of boys from the Park Gang. In many ways Jack was pleased to see them go but when he realized that they had left for good he said: "It's a pity, no one can hold them now." They had been disinterested at first and then became antipathetic. Their antagonism was probably reinforced by the talk of the previous internal constraint. Clothing, too, played an important part in their schism. They were neither interested nor could they afford to keep up with the rapidly changing styles. The present day trend of fashions has underlined the difficult position of the poorer boy to obtain status and acceptance.

The Park Gang's criminals combined with those who had left the Tombstones and were led by an ex-lieutenant. After a short time they were all "down the line" for sentences ranging from three months to two years. All had precious records but for much less serious offences. Moreover on release they were even further removed from the new

adolescent culture, which probably had the result of turning them into
hardened criminals.

The gang also lost the group itself. By this time the group was performing practically every night. There had been a great increase in the
number of dances and the gang soon failed to maintain its following.
The Park Gang did not cease to exist, however. Like most other gangs
it became an organizational centre for going to dances. This shift
towards dancing greatly altered the social rank of girls. One needed a
girl to dance with and steady pairs began to develop. A girl, for
the boy who had passed through the gang's evolution, was a vital
frame of reference before he found his feet as an independent
individual.

Pairing off was paralleled by the external influence of the growth of
beat clubs. The first such club was in Liverpool: The Cavern. This
palatial hole with perspiring walls became the prototype. Boy meets, or
takes, girl in a dampy, hot sticky atmosphere with very little light
anywhere apart from the stage. The beat is important but the atmo-
spherics are all-important.

It became clear that, for any gang, rearranged in this pattern, fighting
would be out of the question. No gang was large enough to monopolize a club and therefore, in the beginning, had to mix with the
remnants of at least three other gangs every visit. In a very small space
of time the boy fighting came to be regarded as just a man without a
woman.

One evening the Tremoloes went to a Liverpool club to listen to a
new and popular group. We were by then playing a combination of
rock and rhythm-and-blues with a heavy pounding bass. We remarked
that although the group on stage made less noise they had more power.
Soon it was noticed that on stage there was a bass cabinet (amplifier)
that was 6 feet high with two huge speakers. We realized that we
needed one of those coffins. Two weeks later the bass amplifier was
ready for a trial. Even on the backing of soft chords there was a terrific
pounding from the box. Immediately the group started to adapt its
regular number to accommodate an accentuated beat. Many groups
had done this before the Tremoloes and within a year it was to become
standard practice on Merseyside. As the bass note was bashed the
drummer did the same and the whole line-up of guitars stamped and
shouted. It was wild and basic. The sound so appealed to us that we,
like others, built the music around the bass notes. The Tremoloes had

achieved what came to be known as the Mersey beat. Playing this style is exhilarating and almost hypnotic. There is the inevitability of the next crashing beat and a terrific climax at the end of each number.

This thumping sound made the clubs relatively complete as the new adolescent world, a new whole source of status within themselves. Adolescents had a music, a number of dances and a "place of their own".

ISOLATION OF THE CRIMINAL

The last 10 years have seen a constantly changing adolescent culture on Merseyside. Gangs are now only for the very young adolescent and the "criminal". These are the two sections of the adolescent world that either cannot or refuse to join in the beat club existence. The average age of beat club attendance seems to be coming progressively lower and a noticeable hierarchical segregation is appearing between the younger and older clubs.

Groups have become adolescents apart. They are symbolic in the widest sense but are really more concerned with professional considerations. Since 1960 there have been over 300 groups on Merseyside. These groups have three common factors: their instability, their steady girls, and their van.

When the group was the symbol of a gang it was almost impossible to disband or discard a member. Now small disagreements after playing every night for four weeks can lead to ugly scenes and break-up. The boy has only one thing he's sure of: his girl. The vehicle is essential as no group plays at one club all night. The group goes on a circuit arranged by a promoter and visits probably three dance halls.

The enormous capital outlay (£130 for each amplifier, £75 for guitars) will keep a new group in poverty for six months and this is the biggest source of discontent. Modern groups change hands—managers, agencies, members, styles and circuits very quickly; probably because they have only the incentive of cash. The whole culture is run, in one respect, as a commercial enterprise with groups as the middlemen.

Perhaps the biggest detrimental effect of change was the isolation of the criminal. Without the gang and its constraint, without the clothing and its in-group connotations, this type of boy has little help, guidance or sympathy from his own age group. This boy has only youth clubs left to help him find his feet. The youth club may well be by-passed by the majority of the beat club members but it has a vital service to perform for the criminal.

Just as in the time of gangs, teenagers are solving themselves rather than their problems, leaving the deviant for the wider society to solve.

17
Why Some Prefer CATs
MARY COUPER

4 FEBRUARY 1965

According to the Robbins Report, the proportion of working class students at university was roughly the same in 1961 as before the war. Despite the increase in the total number of university places, larger and more readily available grants, the growth of the proportion of working class children in grammar education and the rise in their parents' earnings, working class students remain about a quarter of the student population of the universities. In absolute terms, more middle class than working class students have made use of the increased opportunities.

This raises the whole question of differences in class attitudes to education, and particularly to higher education. It is not just the limit to the number of places which prevents more working class students from attending university. It appears to be assumed by those who emphasize the need for more university places of the traditional type and bemoan the small proportion of working class students at university, that this is the form of higher education to which most able young people aspire and which the community both wants and needs. But these assumptions reflect middle class valuations of education; they are not necessarily those of all able young people from working class homes, or of their parents.

Middle class students and their parents may value higher education in its own right, rather than only as a means to a piece of paper which will be the key to an occupational door. For working class youth it is more generally a means to an economic end. In this increasingly qualification conscious society, middle class youth may consider university education a normal step in maintaining the status given them by their families, but for working class young people it is an unusual step involving rise in status—an incentive in itself for some, but by no means for all. Against this are weighed more immediate considerations such as the money the student could be earning, possible courtships and early marriages and the pressures of group solidarity. University education involves long term aims and plans—actual careers cannot be started for at least three years—and long term thinking tends to be a middle class rather than working class characteristic.

A recent study of students at the Bristol College of Science and Technology indicates that working class youth may more easily enter upon a sandwich course at a CAT than the more conventional university form of higher education with its middle class image and less immediate career orientation. The sandwich course, with its industrial placements, suggests work and is by its very nature a job training. Many of the students have the added security of being industry based, of gaining sponsorship by a specific firm as well as a place at college. These features make the courses closer to the experience of people from working class homes and more in accord with the norms of the skilled working class.

Of the Diploma in Technology students at the college, just under one-third in 1963 came from middle class homes, just over two-thirds from working class homes. This would appear to reflect more closely the class distribution in England and Wales as a whole than that found in universities, although it does in fact mask an under-representation of the children of semi-skilled and unskilled workers, with a compensating slight over-representation of the children of skilled manual workers. The picture becomes even more interesting when it is seen that two-thirds of the students were eligible to apply for university places, but that less than half of those eligible had in fact applied. There was little difference between the eligibility of the two class groups, but whether the eligible student applied to a university was closely related to his social class: although only about a third of those eligible for university came from middle class homes, far more middle class than working class students applied to a university. Of those students who did apply to university, over two-thirds either withdrew their applications or turned down a university place. Only 13 per cent of those Diploma in Technology students at the college who had the qualifications to go to university had come to a CAT because they were unsuccessful in their attempts to enter a university. Apparently a large body of students prefer to enter a CAT rather than a university, and many would not have followed any form of full time higher education had a sandwich course not been available.

SUSPICION OF UNIVERSITIES

By far the most important factor influencing young people's attitudes to higher education is the attitudes of their parents. For all Diploma in Technology students at college whose parents had encouraged them to continue their education (nearly two-thirds of the total), the attitude of their parents had been the major influence in their choice to enter higher education. On the other hand, for many of those students whose parents were apathetic about college education the home influence had been equally strong, so that they chose to go to work on leaving school. Many of these students had gone through schools without forming any aspiration for higher education, although they had been aware that the schools wished their pupils to continue to higher education. On leaving school, they had gone straight to work and only after experience at work, where they met graduates, saw the value of qualifications and in some cases gained confidence in their ability to undertake such a course, had they come on to college. For those students whose parents had not encouraged them to continue their education, school influences were seldom strong enough to create this ambition in the student. When a wish for higher education eventually emerged, very few of these students without parental support applied to universities, although some were very well qualified to do so.

There was a marked difference between the proportion of students from working class and middle class homes whose parents had encouraged them to undertake a course of higher education. Whereas a large proportion of the middle class students came to college with their parents' encouragement, just less than half the students from working class homes had this backing, a few of them having parents who were not just apathetic, but actively opposed to higher education for their children. Where working class parents did support their children's wish for higher education, this did not necessarily extend to support for university education. As one student put it, his parents "were suspicious of universities"; the CAT was in keeping with their wish that their son should continue his education and gain a qualification "without the stigma of a university".

By the time he is 15 years old, the student will have begun to make the choices of subject that may lead to his higher education and is also at the age when he may begin to think about leaving school. Some of his friends may have already left school. The Bristol survey showed that, at this stage, while the majority of middle class students were aiming not only at higher education but specifically at university, less than half the working class students had considered continuing to any form of higher education, and of these very few were aiming at winning university entrance.

Another barrier also exists for the potential working class student: he lacks the confidence associated with familiarity with people who had been to university. Only about 10 per cent of the students had parents with a higher education, and all of them were middle class students with parents who had encouraged them to continue their education. It is clear that many students felt unsure about embarking on a course of higher education, largely because no one within the family or immediate circle had undergone such an experience before. Lack of experience also bred ignorance of opportunities, procedures and requirements, many of the students only later becoming aware of the extent of this limitation. More than one student was aware of that working class barrier of lower verbal fluency—as one put it "university people are more articulate" than the students who came to a CAT.

There is also a more positive factor: the "job training" bias and work image of the courses give them an attraction for young people, who in response to the pressures of the norms of that part of society in which they have grown up, would not have been prepared to spend the time on a less job orientated university course. "Education is training for a job", said one student, any other study being "wrong after 16 or 17—a chap should do that in his spare time". The sandwich course was an activity that made sense in terms of the cultural norms of skilled working class, whereas the more abstract concept of "education" was less meaningful.

The fact that this image makes the college and course of study more compatible than a university with the home culture of the working class student was borne out by such remarks as "a university is the tops but for other people" and "university is beyond me and the background I was brought up in". "I fit in here", echoes the remarks of many students. This appeared to be borne out by the relationships of the students with their parents. One might expect a slightly larger number of strained relationships between students and their parents in working class families than in middle class families, as the working class students are undertaking the larger step in terms of social status of occupation; and one might also expect such relationships to be further strained where the student is at college without the support of his parents. In fact there was no evidence that either working class or unsupported students had more strained relations with their parents than other students. Indeed one student said that he had a better relationship with his family now that he "had left a middle class school".

Robbins reports the unchanging proportion of working class students at university, the continued middle class dominance—features which in themselves present an image of a middle class institution preventing many working class students from entering this form of education. The study of the CAT shows that it is an institution with a different image which working class students are able to accept. The majority of these students were eligible to apply for university places but unwilling to go there, the others having equivalent ability but many being without the qualification needed for university entrance because they had not aimed at that goal. The work association of the sandwich period of the course and its job orientation are closer to the experience and values of the student and his parents—one student said his parents "think this is part of the job", whereas for some a university was "snobbish and intellectual", not a place to which to aspire.

Next year the Bristol CAT will receive its University Charter and it is of interest to speculate whether this change in status and title will affect its attractiveness to those potential students who find the existing universities less acceptable. The established image of the college may be further broken by the change in its location from Bristol to Bath. But the sandwich type of course, integrating college learning with practical experience in the work situation, remains the basic form of undergraduate course offered by the new university, and this job training image of the courses may still make them attractive to students who would value less highly the traditional university course.

18
Students in Overalls
ALAN HANCOCK and
JOHN WAKEFORD
14 JANUARY 1965

The great educational divide comes at 15. At that age over half our children leave the educational system for good, and a further quarter stay on at school, in search of qualifications and entry to professional or academic courses. Between these two groups lies another quarter of our young people. They leave school at 15 or 16, but continue to spend a significant part of their time in further education, in full time or part time study. The majority of them are in technical colleges, in particular the local and area colleges. In 1962 there were three quarters of a million enrolments in the major further education establishments by students of 18 or under (about 7 times the university population). Yet in spite of their number they are an unknown quantity.

It is in the local and area colleges that the real core of non-university level technical education for the younger student is found. There are over 500 of these colleges in England and Wales, providing a variety of courses from GCE O and A level subjects, through commercial studies and City and Guilds examinations, up to the Ordinary National Certificate. In 1962, of the 771,000 students under 21, 11 per cent were full time, 36 per cent attended in the evening only and 53 per cent were on day release.

Home Centred

The majority of these students are on vocational courses, basically oriented towards industry. There are far more boys than girls: a ratio of over 4 : 1. Their numbers are increasing; day release has multiplied tenfold since the war (even though the recent report of the Henniker-Heaton Committee emphasizes that day release needs to be doubled by the end of this decade if it is to match 4 per cent growth).

Recently, in preparing for a series of programmes in elementary sociology, designed to help with the teaching of General Studies in these colleges, the BBC mounted a questionnaire survey, examining the family backgrounds, habits and attitudes of 2,500 students. The result is a profile of the Young Technicians—a sizeable proportion of the teenage group, but very different from the lurid case histories of *Generation X*. It is based on a sample of 250 students from each of 10 technical colleges and colleges of further education in England and Wales.

These students are very different from their sophisticated counterparts in higher education. For them adolescent rebellion is not smoothed over by taking courses away from home: the vast majority live with their parents and travel each day from home to work and college. Indeed, their outlook is home centred: most of the time they get on well with both parents. In contrast to university students they identify very little with their college, and far more with the home. Nearly two thirds said that they would first turn to a parent if they were in serious trouble, and under 1 per cent would approach a college tutor.

They come from homes where a rising standard of living is jealously guarded. In a high proportion of cases (50 per cent) the mother either goes out to work or does paid work at home. Forty per cent of them live in privately owned homes (more than in council property), and two thirds have lived at their present address for over five years. Socially they are widely spread (7 per cent from Class 1 homes, 17 per cent from Class 2, 53 per cent from Class 3, 17 per cent from Class 4 and 6 per cent from Class 5). The distribution is close to that of the population as a whole, with only a few more from Class 1 and less from Class 5 than in the national picture.

Their educational history before attending college is again similar to the national picture. The majority come from secondary modern schools (64 compared with a national figure of some 56 per cent), but 7 per cent come from private schools (national figure 6 per cent) and 16 per cent from grammar schools (national average 18·5 per cent). The full time students are, however, much more likely to have a background of private education than those on day release.

The division between full time and day release students is the real crux of the problem, as lecturers working in the colleges know well enough. The major difficulty in technical education is to create a genuine educational environment for students coming in just one day a week. Among the full time students the boys and girls are in roughly equal numbers; the majority of them are on academic or general courses; they are far more likely to have attended a grammar or a private school; they are less likely to live in council property, and in general they come from a higher social background. For them the college can represent a genuine community: 50 per cent of full time students are members of one or more college club, compared with only 8 per cent of day release. Satisfaction with the college is in proportion to the amount of time spent in it. Many of the day release students did not ask to attend the college and are not particularly anxious to stay there. More than half felt that what they did at college could be more closely related to their work. It was only in the smaller colleges that the part time students were more involved with college life: with only one exception membership of college clubs among the day release students was in inverse proportion to the size of the college.

Most of the students from industry are attached to a firm, and over half are apprentices or trainees. Mainly they come from engineering or allied industries, the majority either from very large firms (over 10,000 employees) or from very small firms (less than 100 employees). Eighty per cent of them obtained day release through the firm, and very few through the Youth Employment Service. The majority enjoy their work at least moderately, but already one in four would rather be doing a different job. For them the most important factors in a job are good pay and interesting work, followed by security and opportunities for promotion. They attach little importance to the social standing of a job, responsibility or the opportunity to take decisions.

Trade unionism touches them very little. Of the third who are members of a trade union, well over a half never attend union meetings.

Our sample confirmed Crowther's observation that clubs and formal associations play only a small part in the lives of young people. Outside the college a quarter of the students do not belong to any kind of club. Sports, dancing and jazz clubs are the most popular—each claiming 25 per cent—and youth clubs claim over a third. The uniformed organizations (e.g. Scouts) have only 7 per cent.

In contrast to the impressions of newspaper publicity, the majority never bet or gamble and only a few smoke heavily. There is little drinking apart from the occasional beer. Cinemas, dance halls and coffee bars claim a weekly visit from a third of the students—but 43 per cent have never visited a theatre, 60 per cent an art gallery, and 77 per cent a classical concert.

Their incomes are mostly modest. After tax and insurance deductions, the majority of the regular wage earners are earning between £3 and £7 a week. They give their parents between £1 and £3, leaving them with up to £2 at 16, up to £3 at 17, £4 at 19 and £5 at 20. Here is another, emphatic contrast between the day release and full time students: the non-wage earners have less than £1 a week for themselves.

As expected, the vast majority have television at home, but contrary to the general belief, over half watch more than five hours of television a week. The picture of moderation is continued with record buying: 35 per cent never buy records and another 42 per cent only occasionally.

Most of them read a daily paper (but this is usually the paper available at home, with the *Daily Mirror* and the *Daily Express* firmly in the lead). A surprising 11 per cent read the *Sunday Times*, and an even more surprising 86 per cent regularly read a local newspaper. Books are no part of their lives. Nearly half do not own a single book, and only a third read books outside their studies. A third have never bought a paperback.

Two thirds subscribe, at least nominally, to a belief in God. Only 8 per cent definitely do not believe, and in contrast to university students the percentage of believers is greatest among the older students. The vast majority want to marry in church, with the girls almost unanimous about this. Church attendance, though, is a different matter: a third never go to church and only 20 per cent go weekly (the girls being noticeably more devout).

Politically they are in line with national opinion, with Labour taking a modest lead (their political allegiances reflect the results of public opinion polls conducted at the same time as this survey). Most of their attitudes seem to derive from their parents, rather than from their own thought: they are in favour of restricted immigration and against mixed marriage, opposed to further nationalization, uninvolved in CND, emotionally drawn to the trade unions but practically untouched, in favour of the death penalty, inclined towards flogging and birching, content with the police and the penal system, critical of the churches and in favour of the monarchy.

RESISTING EDUCATION

This is only a brief summary of first results, but it does highlight many of the difficulties of technical education. These colleges have full and part time students working side by side, and the difference between them is sharply etched. The full time student comes to college every day, from a higher social and cultural background, and he is quickly integrated into college life. The day release student is more identified with his home and job: for him college life is marginal. He is more interested in the practicalities of work: he resists education. The college is often an alien society, run by the full time students for their own benefit.

At times, teaching day release students is a desperate and depressing affair. Yet it is a challenge that has got to be met, and, if the results of this survey are anything to go by, the technical college environment may be more fertile than many suppose. Taking the student population as a whole, the number of students from private or grammar school backgrounds is unexpectedly high, suggesting that the colleges may be providing material for an important experiment in social mixing.

In every way these young technicians are a cross section of 15 to 18 year olds. They are not particularly delinquent, or questioning, or literate, or mature. They will make up the "respectable" middle classes of the future, settling at the point where British society thickens round the middle. They may be unenthusiastic about being in college: in the words of one day release student, "It's a waste of time really. You come to college and they tell you to do things one way—you go back to work and they tell you to do it different . . . I'd rather be at work."

Yet as automation develops their importance will increase. Very little is known about the colleges, their relationship with industry, about the students themselves. As the Crowther Survey showed, the

19
New Facts on Teenage Marriage

GRISELDA ROWNTREE

4 OCTOBER 1962

The twentieth century trend towards earlier marriage, which is occurring in all advanced industrial countries, has meant that an increasing proportion of all brides marry before their twentieth birthdays. In Britain, it has risen from 10 per cent in the 1930s to 30 per cent in the 1960s. Some contemporary moralists look askance at this trend, commenting gloomily that early marriages are "shot-gun" marriages and doomed to end in divorce. There is a small element of truth in these jeremiads in that teenage brides are more likely than older ones to be pregnant at marriage and their marriages more liable to break, but these adverse characteristics feature in only a minority of all cases of teenage wedlock. A far greater proportion are a success.

The supporting evidence for this assertion has been assembled by analysing the relevant figures published by the Registrar General and supplementing them with a report on some of the findings of a national inquiry into marriage among persons married during the last 40 years. This survey has been carried out by the Population Investigation Committee in collaboration with the Gallup Poll. In the winter of 1959-60 experienced interviewers questioned about 3,000 men and women aged between 16 and 59 years and living in all parts of Britain. These 3,000 persons, who amounted to 82 per cent of all those selected for study, were found to be a representative cross section of their age range in the national population. In this article the 148 Survey marriages of the 1950s in which the brides were under 20 years of age will be compared with the 393 Survey marriages, also of the 1950s, in which the brides were 20-24 years old, i.e. belonged to the age group which, in spite of earlier wedlock, is still the most popular one for marriage.

First we should mention some characteristics of the teenage brides: following long established custom, the middle and white collar classes, having a more extended education and arriving later at their maximum earnings, tend to marry at older ages than their manual worker contemporaries. The group of Survey marriages with teenage brides has in consequence slightly more of a working class composition than the contrasted group of older ones. To specify: more of the teenagers had fathers of unskilled labouring status, and more of them had been educated just at non-selective, secondary modern, types of schools, had worked before marriage in unskilled and factory jobs, and had married men with similar backgrounds to their own, who also relatively often followed manual occupations. These grooms, though on average 4 years older than their brides, were, of course, younger than the men who married 20-24 year olds.

Although there is this working class bias, it would be a mistake to conclude that *all* our young brides came from the lowest, least skilled, sections of the community. They were in fact widely dispersed, as were the older ones, among the different social groups, at least a quarter of them having a middle class or white collar background. Teenage marriage is not exclusively a lower class habit even though it does involve proportionately rather more girls of unskilled worker parentage.

Nor, as already mentioned, is teenage marriage exclusively "forced" marriage induced by the brute fact of pregnancy alone. The actual situation varies and is in most cases not nearly so sordid as this. A truer perspective on extra-marital pregnancies of all kinds can be built up from the Registrar General's figures which show that in England and Wales in any one year of the 1950s under 2 per cent of all teenage girls (whether married or single) and under 3 per cent of all women in their early twenties had what are called "extra-maritally conceived maternities", i.e. were either pregnant at marriage or gave birth to a child out of wedlock.

Among the brides of any one year the proportion who are pregnant at marriage is, of course, higher. Since the Population (Statistics) Act of 1938 the Registrar General for England and Wales has shown that in each year of the 1950s (as also in 1939) about 27 per cent of all teenage brides, and a lower proportion, around 15 per cent, of those in their early twenties, have been pregnant at their weddings. It is perhaps worth mentioning here that the most recent figures published (for 1962) suggest that an increase is now occurring in these hitherto very stable and unchanging proportions.

The survey results (based, of course, on small numbers and drawn from the whole of Great Britain) more or less parallel the English pattern: 31 per cent of Survey teenage briges, and 13 per cent of the older ones were pregnant at marriage. Conversely, the great majority, i.e. 69 per cent of the teenagers and as many as 87 per cent of the older brides were not; they were on the contrary "prudent" in the sense that by refraining from sexual intercourse before marriage or by other means they had avoided prenuptial pregnancy—or, if not, had deceived the interviewers with complete success.*

In spite of small numbers the Survey data permit some comparisons between the 46 pregnant and the 102 "prudent" among the teenage brides. As in the national population the pregnant brides were on average younger than the "prudent"; over half were not yet 19, the age at which three-quarters of the "prudent" chose to marry. The pregnant showed few distinctive social or educational characteristics. Their predicament—or perhaps the attitude of the churches to it—seems to have led most of them to avoid white weddings and many to solemnize marriage at a Register Office, but it did not prevent them from holding wedding receptions.

So far as their courtships were concerned, it would *not* be correct to assume that their marriages typically followed from casual pick-ups and very short acquaintances. Circumstances varied widely. Admittedly, more of the pregnant had first met their future husbands, not in the popular dance hall, but through encounters at work or in the street. Nevertheless, 54 per cent, as compared with no more than 60 per cent of the "prudent" had known their husbands for at least 18 months before marriage and one-third of both the pregnant and the

---

* The survey informants were not asked directly about pre-nuptial conceptions. The fact was established later by calculating, as the General Register Office does, the interval between the dates given for the marriage and for the first birth. All wives having children within 8½ months of their weddings were allocated to the "pregnant brides" category. This also included several cases in which the exact dates of marriage and/or of the first birth were not recorded but where a pre-nuptial pregnancy was suspected.

"prudent" had had engagements or "understandings" lasting for more than a year. Really short engagements, of 3 months or less, were the lot of only 14 out of the 46 pregnant (i.e. less than one-third, as against one-fifth of the "prudent") and it was probably these 14 at most who were forced into marriage by the fact of pregnancy alone. The other 32 had at least been "going steady" for many months with their fiancés or very special boy friends. In such situations, pregnancy doubtless brought forward the date of the wedding; it can hardly have been the sole factor inducing the couple to marry.

Thus, on the subject of pre-marital conception the Survey showed that less than one-third of the teenage brides of the 1950s were pregnant at marriage. It suggested too that even when pregnant many of them were precipitated into marriages which they would eventually have entered into anyway. It would seem that not more than about one-tenth of all teenage brides had marriage forced upon them by the fact of pregnancy alone.

Whether the brides were pregnant or "prudent", teenage marriages followed from shorter courtships and were not elaborately celebrated so often as those where the brides were in their early twenties. The younger couples also ran into marital adjustment problems—or, at least, admitted to them—slightly more often than the older ones. The percentages reporting any marital adjustment difficulties were 59·5 per cent among marriages with teenage brides, and 51·1 per cent among marriage with brides aged 20-24. The most widespread difficulty was, of course, related to housing.

The great majority of all Survey informants thought that separate and independent accommodation was a major prerequisite for modern marriage, but at the date of interview over a quarter (28 per cent) of our young couples were still living in the same dwelling as one or other of their parents; in this respect they were only a little worse off than the older couples, among whom as many as one-fifth were still living in the parental house. Actual sharing arrangements varied, of course; some couples had been able to establish near-independence while others continued to live just as ordinary members of the wider household. Significant differences appeared between the younger and the older couples in the degree of independence actually achieved, whether under the parental roof or elsewhere. One-tenth of the teenagers, as against only one-twentieth of the older couples said that they had not found "a place of their own yet", and at the other extreme another tenth only of the youngsters as compared with a quarter of their elders had been lucky enough to find independent self-contained accommodation at the start of marriage. In between were the majority of both the younger and the older couples who had either obtained semi-independence in furnished or shared accommodation right from the beginning or had secured some measure of domestic independence only later.

More of the teenage couples (i.e. about one half of them) had to wait at least a year after marriage before they acquired any degree of independence at all. In this way they were more often victims of the general housing shortage than their elders. In cases, where, as well as being young, the bride was also pregnant, couples seem to have been less successful than their contemporaries in getting some degree of independence by the date of their often hurried weddings, but numbers are too small to show statistically significant differences. In the 1950s fairly full employment provided the opportunity, and the high cost of setting up home one incentive, for brides to continue to earn after marriage. Just over half of the Survey teenagers, as compared with almost two-thirds of the older brides, stayed at work, the young brides' lower employment rate being associated in part with their never having worked at all, and more importantly with the higher incidence among them of pre-nuptial pregnancy. There were other factors positively affecting decisions to continue working. For instance, among the "prudent" teenagers who still had no children by the date of interview, over four-fifths (82 per cent) had carried on with their jobs, as had almost as many (77 per cent) of the corresponding group of older brides. Some working wives were, of course, only very recently married and would probably leave their jobs as they started to have children, but others among both the teenage and the older brides intended to go on earning for some time and had consequently adopted contraceptive practices right from the beginning of marriage. These working brides who took deliberate steps to postpone childbirth constituted only a minority in each of our age groups: they were no more than 22 per cent of all teenagers, but as many as 35 per cent of the older women.

The Survey indicated some further similarities and contrasts between the two age groups with respect to the early stages of family building. About three-quarters of our couples (all married in the 1950s) had had at least one child by the date of interview; more of the teenagers than of the older brides had started their families, and there is some slight indication that among those married in the early 1950s more of the young brides had gone on to have at least a second baby before their fifth wedding anniversaries. The youngsters' more rapid rate of family-building was, of course, associated with their more frequent pre-nuptial pregnancies: where the "prudent" alone were concerned, there was no significant difference between the older and younger couples in the proportions who had any children.

Nevertheless, fewer of the "prudent" youngsters had used birth control right from the start of their marriages; only 39 per cent had done so as against 55 per cent of their "prudent" elders. They did, however, almost catch up after the birth of their first child, and by the date of interview as many as three-quarters of both the young and the older "prudent" couples had adopted contraception. There were also by this date similar proportions of birth controllers (i.e. around 75 per cent) among those of each age group who had been pregnant at marriage. Thus, whether teenage or older, whether pregnant or "prudent", a substantial majority of our mid-century couples had begun at quite early stages in their married lives to use contraception as a means of controlling and spacing their family's growth.

In many of the respects examined here teenage marriages appeared to differ little from older ones. There were, of course, minor differences. The youngsters seemed at first glance rather less deliberate and far-sighted: even the "prudent" among them apparently did not wait to get a home of their own before marrying so often as their elders did and fewer adopted birth control right from the start of married life. It is possible, however, that these differences were more closely associated with the working class bias of the teenage group than with their youth. Working class couples are less adequately housed than middle class ones, and fewer of them start birth control at marriage, but our Survey numbers are too small to allow us to disentangle satisfactory class, as distinct from age, influences on behaviour. In these circumstances it would be unfair to condemn at least the "prudent" youngsters for lack of forethought when in fact they may merely be copying the pattern of behaviour set by their social equals.

The Survey material carried no indication at all that the "prudent" who marry young deliberately postpone their first birth for a longer period than their elders. While the relationship between early marriage and exceptionally frequent child-bearing may with the spread of birth control have weakened still further since this long term trend was first shown in the Family Census of 1946, our teenage brides are still relatively fertile in at least the early years of their married lives; they start their families more quickly and apparently build them more rapidly than their elders. This may be due to a genuine philoprogenitive preference for parenthood among the young, but their higher rate of pre-nuptial pregnancy and the "prudents'" lesser use of birth control from the start of married life suggest that it may also be associated with their relative ignorance of, or reluctance to adopt, effective contraception before and immediately after marriage.

What are the prospects for making a success of teenage marriage? At the start, the young couples are likely to be rather worse housed and soon become rather more encumbered with children than their elders. These facts may help to explain why national figures published only since the mid-1950s show that marriages with teenage brides run, at each duration, about twice the risk of ending in divorce as those of brides in their early twenties. Even with this much greater risk, however, these figures suggest that over 80 per cent of all teenage marriages will remain intact and unbroken as compared with more than 90 per cent of those with the older brides.

A few questions were asked in the Survey about marriage breakdown, but it is too soon to estimate its ultimate extent among the couples studied here, of whom none had been married for more than 10 years and some for only a very short period. Of the Survey marriages of earlier decades, which were, of course, subject to the exceptional strains and stresses of economic depression and of war, the rather rare teenage, and especially the even rarer pregnant teenage, marriages were more liable to divorce or separation than those of older couples. But even in these earlier disturbed decades, about four-fifths of the relatively vulnerable young marriages remained unbroken. On the evidence so far available it looks as if post-war marriages in general are less likely to end in divorce than those of the war or just pre-war years. It may well be that there are today even better prospects for success in teenage marriage than there have been in the recent past.

20
Young Marriage
PAUL BARKER

17 SEPTEMBER 1964

You will see them in your High Street this Saturday. She carries the shopping bag; he manoeuvres the Silver Cross. While the wife goes into the dry cleaners, her husband joggles the pram handle up and down. The baby is a few weeks old. Its parents also are young, perhaps only 19. They seem to be enjoying themselves. The sight is the sign of a new social phenomenon, but not quite the one that most observers seize on. Young marriage in 1964 is mainly the story of the teenage (or thereabouts) husband.

Forget about teenage brides. There are more of them than there used to be—two and a half times as many as in 1938. But they aren't a novelty. Already before the war more than 1 bride in 10 was a teenager. Young husbands, by contrast, are a genuine innovation. The change in ratio is fantastic. Five pre-war brides married under 21 for every underage groom. In the 1950s, the ratio was down at 4 to 1; now it is 3 to 1, if not lower. The corollary is that there are more very young *couples*. At least 10 per cent of marriages are between minors. Even if a girl before the war married young, her husband married old.

All the advanced industrial countries are experiencing this shift towards earlier marriage. Economics is an important cause. Jobs for almost everybody and good wages for the young mean that a big barrier is gone; and irregular work with poor pay deterred men more than women: they had to support the family. Full employment has helped the blue collar workers rather than the traditional white collar men. (It has only made insurance clerks dissatisfied at having security as their job's apparent chief reward.) And young weddings are more characteristically proletarian than bourgeois. So the best place to check on how they work out is a district like South London around Camberwell: where ordinary people live but the pattern of life isn't complicated by the Jewishness of Whitechapel or the colouredness of Brixton.

What is the combined impact of a young husband and easier money? How does a young couple's life differ from their unmarried friends'? Do they still see the old gang, or does marriage immerse them? What effects does a child have? And what is the young marrieds' relation to Mum? (Why also have mother-in-law jokes died out?) I had long talks with young couples in and around Camberwell to find out.

None was older than 23, none married longer than 18 months. The husbands' jobs spread from skilled work like printing to warehouseman or packer. All the couples except one wife had left school at 15. That wife, who had taken GCE, worked in a bank. She would stop work when she got pregnant. The other wives observed this same divide: they were either mothers/pregnant or else they went out to a job. The job was partly for the money, partly for the interest of it. Some husbands felt it wasn't right for a wife to work but their view didn't win: their age makes them more a companion who advises than a father substitute who commands. Only one pregnant wife, however, was reluctant to cross the divide when the time came. She wanted to be back at work in 2 or 3 years; other girls thought they would wait at least till the children had left school.

GAP IN KNOWLEDGE

For social workers, young marrieds are a curious gap in their knowledge. The couples see as little of them as they often see of their friends. They vanish from the youth clubs and even from the discotheques. The Peckham Disque has only had one married couple back in a year. The people themselves will have to speak. Like Peter Docherty.

Peter is 18, his wife is 21. Their chubby daughter is 9 months old. Peter earns about £16 a week as a plumber's mate. Before she was pregnant, Maureen made tea in a works canteen. Housing plays the biggest part in their plans.

"Jobs are all right now, but not housing. Round here it's diabolical:

a right take on. When we got married we lived in furnished rooms. The bloke there, he's Greek. We paid £4 10s just for 2 rooms. He was willing to sell for £350, but where could we get that? I worked it out he must be making a fortune: they paid £5 10s downstairs, another on the same landing as us paid £2 10s, and upstairs was £4 10s again. He never gave no receipt or rent book. I reckon he was fiddling the tax people."

They live now with Maureen's parents, having the front room, furnished, for their own. The baby sleeps in the grandparents' room "because it's warmer". The Dochertys still pay £4 10s but it includes board. Peter is trying to get a 2 room unfurnished flat in a tenement block. A relative set him on to it. The block is probably due to come down, and he hopes that will mean a council flat. The printers were the only husbands I met who were thinking of a house of their own. Everyone else's ideal was a council tenancy: they moved into condemned property or became lodgers in Mum's council house for the chance of being rehoused.

"We wondered once about going to a New Town," Peter Docherty said. "But we found there was more to it than there seemed. The husband has to be passed by a board, then find lodgings and get a job, before you get a house. I don't think that a reasonable proposition. It put me off. And my wife wasn't keen. I wasn't that keen myself: they want skilled men there, and what use is a £5 10s apprenticeship to me?"

Like Jack Clark, a printer, whose wife offered coffee instead of tea, these husbands' determination was "to earn as much money as I can". Work ambition was fairly limited. A bus conductor wanted to become a driver. A 19 year old soccer professional simply intended to stay in the game as long as they'd let him. Peter Docherty would stay in plumbing, though he hoped for his own business eventually. Even the warehouseman was content with his job: he worked long hours and could sometimes get £30 a week, not all of it passing through the taxman. Most incomes, most weeks, were between £11 and £16.

USE OF MONEY

The money was for the home or for saving. Only couples without children (actual or imminent) spent much outside.

"We don't want a child for about 2 years," Brenda Collier said. She is 22 and gets £8 to £9 a week at the gummed-paper works where her 23 year old husband, John, earns £11 as a packer. They were engaged at 17, "but we felt we were too young to marry; besides, we wanted a nice wedding and didn't want to marry into debt". After 2 years of saving they had their 5 bridesmaid, 80 guest church wedding last spring. (They followed the new etiquette: if you want a big wedding, you help pay for it—usually everything except the caterer.)

We sat drinking tea among the bright flowery wallpaper, the gilt framed mirror, the splay legged furniture. The television, which they had bought outright, was on. In the corner stood a large radiogram. It had been handed on by Brenda's mother, who lived round the corner in a prefab, when she bought a new one. Mum was drinking tea with us. Couples are anxious to start up away from home and be independent: living with in-laws is only a last resort. But they still see a lot of their families. To go there for a cup of tea and a chat is the most frequent outing. Brenda Collier is at her mother's every day.

They had had the flat for a year before they moved in. They took off the encrusted layers of wallpaper, filled the cracks in the plaster, got a carpenter friend to build cupboards over the sink on the landing. They got the whole place furnished in advance. Almost everything was paid for cash down. Only £1 a week goes out in hire purchase, for the bedroom suite and gas cooker.

The Colliers were exceptionally prudent. A local clergyman was probably thinking of them when he said: "The amount that young couples start marriage with amazes me." But others were just as serious minded about home; as averse to hire purchase (£2 10s week was the highest debt); and as determined to have as well equipped a place as they could afford—whether they could find decent premises or not. Living with in-laws generally followed a wedding hastened by pregnancy (sometimes a wedding planned anyway; sometimes, as with the Dochertys, "we couldn't really say if we would have got married without the baby"). But it was a dismal business to find an alternative; and the alternatives themselves could be pretty dismal.

The Langhams live in the tenements that the Dochertys are hoping to move into. It was a block like Islington's Beaconsfield Buildings (where Philip, the husband, was born). A boarded off cellar by the door sent out a repellent stink of drains and tom cats. "We had the sanitary in to have a look at it," Margie Langham said. "But they just put their head in the house and said: 'You've got a lovely home here. There's lots worse off than you.' And went away. It used to be a debtor's prison here in the old days, I've heard. Shakespeare had something to do with it."

In a way the Langhams class as reckless. But not given the economy of the Britain they have always worked in. They spend in the context of money coming in. The house was littered with knick-knacks that Philip had bought for it (some of them got cheap at work). Margie had a 59 guinea washer, alone among the wives I met. "But it's a dreadful machine. I've seen a nice one at 109 guineas. We shall have to get a new suite, too." There was nothing wrong with the red moquette, but it was only a 2 piece. Margie felt it wasn't a real suite without a settee.

The Langham marriage came nearest to a probation officer's opinion that "marriage here is traditionally a battleground". When Margie met me at the door in her curlers, she looked 10 years older than her actual 20. I could hardly talk through the semi-bickering backchat of husband and wife. "Don't want them," Philip said when he came home to the apple pies Margie had baked. "I knew you'd say that," she replied, accepting that men were difficult. Margie spent most of the day out, seeing relatives or old girl friends, but Philip didn't raise a finger to do ordinary chores and wasn't expected to. None the less, home and an old car were his two real interests. He only went to the caff to see his mates if Margie and he had a row.

Most husbands moved cheerfully into helping with the house. Their age has something to do with it. Before marriage their pattern of life is like their wives'; often out, plenty of clothes, lots of entertainment. Then the sudden plunge into either marriage (with a baby) or into saving. After the marriage it is natural that they should want to, or feel they ought to, continue to share the pattern. They enter marriage trailing all kinds of traditional attitudes derived from their parents' homes. ("Conscious rejection doesn't prevent the influence coming through," a psychologist remarked.) Some husbands draw the line at washing up. Some must have one night a week out with the boys. One said "I'm in favour of hitting women, especially if the wife degrades herself" (not that he did). But the Clarks' habit of spending every other Saturday "looking in the shops and dreaming what we shall have when we get a house" points the way forward. Mother-in-law is no longer a joke because son-in-law shares her interest in homemaking.

The first child has a more shattering effect on the premarriage pattern than the wedding itself has. The Colliers live rather how they did before they married: ladies' darts on Tuesdays; men's darts on Thursdays; a drink, a dance or a party on Saturday night. John also goes off to watch Spurs on Saturday. That is his only solo excursion. (Sport, or a trip to the betting shop, is the one all male pastime that survives engagement and marriage.) On the seventh day the Colliers stay in. With a child the routine becomes one night *out* a week, when a grandparent or an unmarried friend of the wife's can babysit. "That's the way the cookie crumbles," one 22 year old husband said, after a week of marriage. But his wife was six months gone and had another child (not his) already. Peter Docherty's dedication to fatherhood was more typical.

He dandled young Carol on his knees and told me all about her teething troubles. He helps to bath her and likes to take her for walks on a Sunday: "it's only a shilling to Regent's Park". He explains: "When you're married and got a little baby, it's something to work for. You've got your responsibilities. Before, I never knew what home was. It was always the all night caffs for me. I'm not all that interested now. The boys are getting married anyway and that." Like Philip Langham he used to be a Rocker. Philip now justifies his car as a way to take the expected baby out. Peter hasn't any transport at the moment: he wants a second hand motor bike; but only, he says, for going to work.

MATURITY FACTOR

Specialists emphasized to me that it wasn't the age in years that counted if a marriage was to work. It was emotional maturity. Young couples could have that as well as older people. The difficulty with some young marriages is that the marriage can be merely a sortie in the war against parents. Which leads to trouble.

In theory, Peter Docherty's marriage might look like that. When the Dochertys are in (i.e. most of the time), they watch television or play the records that they still buy. Sometimes they have friends in. Peter's aunts come round regularly. All this resembles the other couples. But Peter's mother never comes.

"There's lots of hatred in my family. I never got on with my mother. I couldn't miss her. She ran off with my uncle after my father died. I always got on golden with my dad. When he died, I tell you, doctors do cry. It isn't just something you see on the television." Peter was never out of trouble with the police. The baby was born before they married because he was doing time in a detention centre for robbery with violence. But he isn't stupid. In the centre he made sure he earned full remission. "It's meant to be a short sharp shock and it is and all. They have you just like a lot of bleeding sheep: you're not people." He intends to stay clear: next time it would be 3 years.

Marriage, whatever its other virtues, can be at least a short term cure for delinquency. It can even help a 40 year old go straight, a local probation officer said; so it has a still stronger effect on the adaptable young.

Peter was a father to please any marriage counsellor. Maureen was happy enought to shop, housekeep and look after Carol. She didn't mind that she had to wash by hand. Young wives, like young husbands, are resilient. But just as Peter helped with Carol, so it was certain he would make sure Maureen got the vacuum cleaner, fridge and washer she wanted when they found a house of their own—where he would do as much home decorating as other young husbands.

It always comes back to accommodation. The National Marriage Guidance Council have found that in marriages of less than 3 years, living conditions are one of the chief troubles (i.e. symptoms if not diseases) that people come to counsellors with. Infidelity stays near the bottom of the list: this is an older person's reaction to marriage difficulties; it appears near the head of the council's list for marriages more than 18 years old. On both lists income comes last.

The economic circumstances which have produced young husbands have also reduced the prime worry: bread. With that out of the way, young couples are doing their worrying about the roof and the veneer of the sideboard. I was surprised how seldom education—either their own or their children's—was mentioned. But I shouldn't have been. Education is third priority. When the housing problem has gone the way of unemployment, there will be the clamour for education that today, at this level, is lacking. And 18 year olds may have the vote then.

21

A Humanist's Decalogue

RONALD FLETCHER

2 MAY 1963

Do we need a new morality, especially for teenagers? I think not.

The chief need at present is to stop dramatizing our situation; to stop thinking of ourselves as unique and uniquely ill-treated. All the neurotic, apocalyptic talk about the failure of the "old" and the desperate need for the "new" in morality is becoming rather ridiculous.

We pride ourselves on our realism, but we are being presented with a new melodramatic romanticism of the 20th century backstreets: the young "Tough and Tender" confronting the glass and concrete jungle. Byron's "Manfred", facing the evil forces of the spirit world in some craggy tower in the craggy European mountains; Shelley's open-necked youth crying tragedy so beautifully from the soft Italian shores, has now become the lonely teenager, smart-cum-scruffy, leaning against the hard brick wall, tie askew, cancerous fag drooping from the corner of his gob, an insolent urbane leer in his eyes, taking it cool, rejecting the complex constraints and obligations of the world, and with them, the disgusting hypocrisy of the "oldeys"; facing a universe made dull by potted TV astronomy and empty of those exciting myths which gave meaning to the lives of earlier, luckier generations. Off he slouches to smoke a bit of hemp, meet his permissive doll round the corner, dallying with her lovely dyed hair, making a meal of his misery until the bang goes off and the mushroom shaped cloud swallows up his agony.

What a silly caricature it is.

The majority do not come within miles of it; neither do they want to.

To begin with, all the supposed facts which are held to make ours a unique, crucial and generally worsened situation, are, at the very least, highly dubious. It is by no means certain that young people of today are more given to sexual licence, more anti-social, more irresponsible, more apathetic, more confused about moral issues, than young people of earlier times. The several studies of young people (by Thelma Veness, Mr and Mrs Eppel and others) all show that most of them are far less sinister and sensational than this. They appear to have quite modest, sensible aims: they want peace and quiet and happiness and love and a house with a garden and a sandpit at the bottom (not, one would have thought, unique in human history?). They seem to get on quite well with their parents. They do not appear to be continually raging round the streets, foaming at the mouth for casual irresponsible sex, and they seem to be remarkably and sensitively concerned with mutuality of consideration in their personal relationships. Of course, they are worried by the bomb, but who is not?

Many aspects of the social situation are considerably improved today. But the gloomy, ghastly vultures—the companions of doom—cannot be happy unless they have blackened 20th century mankind completely. These croaking vultures will argue that, though some so-called social and material improvements (little things like piped water, baths, lavatories, better health, longer life, more pleasure and less pain) have been made, we are in fact (inwardly) far more wicked than before, and, during the past 50 years, have perpetrated far greater evils than have ever been committed in human history. They will praise earlier, simpler, nobler times and denounce such recent evils as Hilter's treatment of the Jews. But this modern-man-hating myth of the vultures cannot be attacked too hotly.

In the 20th century, the hating, plundering and murdering of Jews by Hitler was repudiated in disgust, horror and sadness by the rest of the world. But throughout the history of Christendom, until the power of the Church was broken (by awful rationalists and revolutionaries) this, though not at all times so violent, was the generally accepted attitude and practice towards the Jews.

No, the world has improved very much during the past 150 years, and men are now in the throes of great difficulties and intense conflicts largely because they have every intention of improving matters still further—and for everyone, not only for the few most fortunate nations.

It is doubtful, too, whether those factors which are held to have changed the nature and social position of the teenager have really raised any new moral issues. It is true that the possibility of nuclear war is a ghastly prospect; but earlier generations have also had to face the threatened disruption of their lives and destruction of their civilizations by war, and though nuclear war would be much more devastating, it is doubtful how far the fear of it really enters into our experience as a deeper emotional factor. Somehow, it is a possibility difficult really to believe. In any case, the threat does not change moral issues.

The idea that the threat of early extinction is a valid excuse for indulging uncontrolled appetites is only a variant of the idea that: "If I knew there was no after life—I should just have a good time. What would be the point of being good?" But such a person has not begun to know what morality is about.

It is true, too, that we live in a complex world which is difficult to alter by political action. Sometimes, therefore, we feel helpless, even apathetic. But this is not a new situation. The institutions of society must always seem a massive set of constraints to the young people who grow up within them, and though it is true that modern society is more complicated than hitherto, it is also true that far greater efforts are now directed to making it clear for young people so that they can be helped towards meaningful social participation and citizenship. Also, young people now have greater opportunities to alter their society than had earlier generations. It must not be forgotten that complete adult suffrage in Britain (for women as well as men) is only 35 years old.

Similarly, though there may be a "gap" between parents and adolescents, this, surely, cannot be greater than in earlier generations? Modern parents, though they may be perplexed as to how to help and advise their children, are so because they are more sensitive to the problems of upbringing and are less confident in the "parental authority" which they are supposed to possess. This should be a ground for greater understanding, not less.

As to sexual morality, it is generally said that improved nutrition and health with earlier maturing, the extension of the period of dependence at school, better education, and the relatively high incomes shortly after school-leaving, have resulted in a great change in sexual behaviour, which raises new moral issues. Certainly these factors are at work, but I strongly suspect that we are exaggerating their effects. I do not think the extent of earlier maturing is so striking as to have made much difference. Children have always matured early enough to make sex a problem. In any case, coupled with the knowledge about earlier maturing, we have also been shown how markedly the rate of maturation differs between individuals. To compare generation with generation is therefore an almost pointless oversimplification.

The increased wealth of teenagers certainly makes for greater independence, but whether this has substantially changed the pattern of sexual behaviour is, again, open to doubt. Before the last war, for example, most youngsters left school at 14, and many left grammar schools at 15 and 16, and, though their wages would not be as high as those of the present day, they certainly used them for similar purposes. I sometimes think I must be the only adult in Britain who remembers the "Monkey Runs" on Sunday evenings before World War II, when young men, wearing the smartest and flashiest suits they could manage to buy (or white silk scarves showing under their belted, military-style macks), prowled up and down the flagstoned pavements in towns and villages alike, casting lewd flirtatious glances and uttering occasional guffaws of embarrassed laughter at the haughty-then-coy-and-giggling-then-straight-away-all-haughty-again girls who were also dressed to kill; and how the sorting out of the gangs and couples went on; and the drifting off to the rough wooden seats along the roadsides, the stiles, the dark fences behind the houses, the woods, the patches of wasteground. . . . Have things changed so much?

Finally, when one stops to think about it, why are all these criticisms levelled particularly at the young? When it is said that the young experience difficulties over sex, that they are morally confused, helpless in the face of large-scale organisation and distant authority, politically apathetic, worred about the bomb, and so on, the implication seems to be that the old ones are different. But are we? The truth is, surely, that every charge, every criticism, every worry that can be voiced against the young at the present time can, with equal validity, be voiced against the rest of us.

There are, also, no new ethical principles that we can conjure out of the blue for our guidance. It is, as is always the case, a matter of applying the ethical principles we already possess to the changed situation in order to be as clear as possible what our conduct ought to be.

Given this sceptical approach, it is very questionable whether I should try to lay down commandments; especially, too, because I believe that young people are capable of working out their own way, and, whether we like it or not, will do so. Indeed, it is an arrogance to assume otherwise.

Still, when in the context of all these criticisms we are asked point-blank by young people: "What ought we to do? What rules of conduct do you offer us?"—we must try to give an answer. It is no use simply arguing the toss in front of them, praising or blaming them, disputing endlessly whether things are getting better or getting worse. At some time, we must face up to their challenge.

Hence the following decalogue. May I say, however, that, unlike Moses, I cannot lay claim to having had conversations with the Almighty, and, perhaps in consequence, I possess neither the certitude of Moses nor his extreme simplicity of mind and utterance.

Ten Non-commandments

1. Never accept authority:

whether that of a jealous god, priest, prime minister, president, dictator, school teacher, social worker, parent, or of anyone else whatsoever, unless, in your own seriously considered view, there are good grounds for it.

You are quite right to reject orthodox religions; at present (as our clergymen insist) orthodox religions are a shambles.

Given the present state of knowledge, the only position of integrity you can hold is one of careful, honest, open-minded agnosticism. Follow a rigorous honesty in all your feelings, thinking and acting.

You may say: "But this, surely, is a position of arrogance? My knowledge about important questions is so little." But this is true of all of us. Those persons who are most authoritative in their subjects are the first to acknowledge the tentative nature of their knowledge and the large areas of their ignorance. It is empty men who are pretentious. Always be suspicious of "experts" and accept nothing they say without radical citicism. *You*, in the last analysis, are the only judge of what seems right and feasible to *you;* therefore question stubbornly until you are satisfied. Be self reliant.

But remember: your position should rest upon your own *seriously considered* point of view. There is a big difference between honest obstinacy and silly insolence.

2. BASE YOUR CONDUCT UPON SIMPLE HUMANE PRINCIPLES:

Try to increase the happiness and diminish the pain in the world.

Always treat other individuals as persons, as ends in themselves. Never use them, manipulate them, exploit them, or in any way treat them only as a means to some end of your own.

Practise reciprocity: behave towards others as you think it right that they should behave towards you.

Recognize the importance of, and seek to preserve, certain fundamental human rights for example: *Liberty*—that all men should be free to pursue what, for them, is a good and enjoyable life, so long as they respect, and do not infringe upon, the same liberty of others: *Equality*— that, though men are by nature different, and in their particular abilities superior and inferior to each other; as whole persons they are not superior or inferior to each other, and are deserving of equal consideration.

Seek also to preserve those other rights which these principles imply; such as full political citizenship, education, health, equality before the law and others of this kind. These rules provide a basis for the regulation not only of your own personal life and relationships, but also of the organization of society.

Some may ask: "But how can we accept these moral rules without divine authority? If we are unsure about the nature, even of the existence, of God—how do we know right and wrong?" The answer is very simple: God has nothing to do with the matter. These rules of conduct are worked out in relation to our own human predicament and in order to resolve our own human disputes, and we decide that they are right and good simply because in human experience, after much heart-searching and reasoning, we find them to be so. They are not in any way weakened because you have no belief in, or have doubts about, any "ultimate authority" such as God.

3. STRIVE TO ELIMINATE WAR:

a variant upon "Thou shalt not kill, in which we agree with Moses.

Sometimes, when things are allowed to go too far, and uncriticized for too long, war, for most people, seems to break out almost unexpectedly. Then millions of people who previously had no evil intentions towards each other are engaged in destroying and ruining each other because, in the circumstances, killing seems necessary and justifiable.

But killing is always foul and repugnant. War is never glorious, though the qualities of character of individuals who endure it may well be. War is one of the most disgusting evils of mankind which now, in addition, has reached the stage of lunacy. You are right to protest against nuclear war. The time has come to do everything in our power to outlaw war completely.

4. STRIVE TO ELIMINATE POVERTY, AND WORK FOR GREATER MATERIAL PROSPERITY FOR ALL:

Poverty is one of the most crushing, deadening, humiliating experiences that can happen to men. If poverty and war could be eliminated, two of the worst scourges of mankind would be gone. Material prosperity is not a sufficient basis of human happiness and fulfilment, but it is a necessary one.

If we take this aim seriously, it means that it is our duty to work hard, efficiently, and in such a way as to contribute the greatest excellence of which we are capable to the community. *Work* is one of the most important things, and, strange though it sounds nowadays, one of the most satisfying things in human experience. To try to achieve the highest qualities of excellence of which you are capable both in what you like doing and in what you are committed to do—being a good nurse, a good carpenter, a good cook, a good driver, a good fitter, a good athlete, a good parent—is as good a basis as any for a satisfying personal life.

5. DO NOT BE A SNOB:

a variant upon "Thou shalt not covet", in which we also agree with Moses. Reject the growing poison of status consciousness and social emulation. Treat people as human beings, and not as competitors with jobs, incomes and material possessions against which you have to be perpetually measuring yourself. Use material possessions for enjoyment and for enriching your own experience: not as an insignia of status for competitive snobbery. Instead of fastening upon some label which separates and distinguishes you from others ("middle class", "public school", "B.A.", "clerk", "foreman", "copy-typist-to-the-manager", "sociologist"), put your common humanity first and your label second. There is something pathetic about a society in which people have to make so much fuss about their labels; it can only be because they are so impoverished in their inner human resources.

Work for a society in which there is more human comradeship, and less pretence.

6. IN SEXUAL BEHAVIOUR—USE YOUR BRAINS AS WELL AS YOUR GENITALS, AND ALWAYS IN THAT ORDER.

Remember, too, that love is more than both. Sex is a natural impulse, an appetite for complete physical, emotional, and mental intimacy, including many sensual delights, and consummated finally in the act of intercourse. As such, there is nothing right or wrong about it, certainly nothing evil, it is an enjoyable experience which we all desire.

Sex is also a powerful appetite, and like other appetites, needs regulation both with reference to other aspects of our own nature, and with reference to our behaviour towards others. It is here that questions of sexual ethics arise; and it is clear that—far from being stuffy or old-fashioned—the ethics of sex are unavoidable and sensible.

The principles in the light of which we ought to regulate our sexual behaviour are exactly the same as those by which we regulate our other behaviour: to treat others as ends in themselves and not only as means to our own gratification; to practise reciprocity; to behave towards others as we think it right that they should behave towards us; to act with regard to our own and other people's happiness and to avoid causing pain. On the basis of these principles what specific rules of sexual behaviour for teenagers can we clarify? It is certain, first of all, that:

Young men and women at and after puberty ought to exercise self-control over their sexual conduct.

At this stage of maturity, sexual need becomes an extremely intense and serious matter. Sex becomes a continuous and powerful appetite which is easily and almost indiscriminately stimulated. In a way different from our other impulses it seems to entail a more complete emotional commitment to another person. Also, sexual intercourse may now have the serious consequence of bringing children into being. At puberty, sexual desires and motives have become more than a matter of play and excitation; they foreshadow a new kind of relationship, intruding upon the old, disrupting the old, more demanding than the old. Control is therefore necessary; carelessness in sex is a fool's game.

Pre-marital sexual experience is not necessarily wrong.

If undertaken with mutual consent, full mutuality of regard, and responsibility, it is difficult to see why—whether in a short-lived relationship or in an affair of longer duration—the mutual enjoyment of sexual experience for its own sake between two unmarried people is wrong.

Much care should be exercised about this kind of sexual relationship, however. It is very doubtful whether many adolescents can enter easily into such casual sexual adventures. Sex is not a simple appetite which can be satisfied by the acquisition of an object (as, when one is hungry, one can eat a meal); it is a complex desire which carries with it profound emotions and the likelihood of profound emotional attachment which may involve people far more deeply than they had expected. It needs the exercise of much forethought, lest something that begins lightly should end in suffering.

There is another kind of pre-marital sexual relationship which entails full, mutual commitment and responsible consideration. In the context of all the factors of contemporary society we have mentioned, there may be some young people who, ultimately intending to marry, may think it wiser to delay their marriage. They may, however, wish to enter into sexual intimacy meanwhile. This kind of pre-marital relationship is not wrong.

Many objections are likely to be made to this position. It will be said that promiscuity results in the continued spread of venereal disease and the large number of illegitimate births. Pre-marital sex as I have described it is by no means the same thing as undiscriminating promiscuity. Even so, the answer to this objection is clear. Young people (and others) should be given a thorough knowledge of venereal disease so that it can, as far as possible, be eradicated and avoided. Similarly, they should be given a thorough knowledge of contraceptive techniques so that they may avoid having children they do not want, and for whom they cannot properly care.

It may also be said that, in the serious, fully committed kind of pre-marital relationship, no matter how sincere and convinced young people may be, they may have made a great mistake. They may find, in fact, that they are profoundly unhappy together, and may be led, therefore, to end their relationship. But what is wrong with this? If a mistake can be made in this kind of relationship—*so can a genuine and profound mistake be made in marriage.* And surely it is better to know this before, rather than after, the full obligations of the founding of a family have been entered into?

It may be said that the short or long-lived affair and even the supposedly serious pre-marital relationship are wrong because deception and irresponsibility can occur, and one partner may be treated as a means only, and exploited for the gratification of the other. There is a curious flaw in this objection. It is agreed that irresponsibility and calculated deception makes any such relationship wrong; but the object seems glibly to assume that once you are *married* these moral evils somehow disappear. The lion of sex is safely locked in, and you can forget about him now. What a preposterous argument this is! The idea that all sexual experience within marriage is necessarily all right, simply *because* it is *within* marriage, and that all sexual experience outside marriage is all wrong, simply *because* it is *outside* marriage, is nonsense. It is just as possible to treat your wife, or husband, as a means to your own gratification; to deceive them and exploit them to your own ends—rather than giving them full consideration as a person—as it is to treat anyone else in this way. Indeed, it may well be easier. An important point arises from this:

We should concern ourselves as much with the ethics of sexual relationships within marriage as with those outside it.

And it is a very odd thing, when you stop to consider it, that people should always be so anxious about the morality of pre-marital and extra-marital sex, but seldom raise seriously the question of sexual morality *within* marriage.

Extra-marital sexual experience is not necessarily wrong.

For some married couples, sexual fidelity is part of the shared ideal of their marital relationship; indeed, of their ideal of love. Sexual infidelity is therefore a deception, a breach of faith and confidence, a breaking of the relationship.

For other couples, sexual fidelity is not part of the ideality of their marital relationship. For them, there can be an honest understanding on the part of both that (perhaps not always, but at certain periods, at certain ages, given certain circumstances, and so on) they desire wider sexual experience, and an open agreement that they should both enjoy it. This may be possible simply because their relationship is so secure. Again it is not the fact of having sexual desire for others which makes the situation right: it is the fact that there is no deception.

Having come to the end of these rules concerning sex—reject them,

subject them to radical criticism, think again, and again, and again. . . .
No subject is more complex; for no other subject is it more difficult to
lay down rules.

7. ENJOY FAMILY LIFE AND MARRIAGE:

Approach your own marriage very carefully; bearing in mind the
many serious obligations into which you are entering, both with
regard to your partner, and, particularly, with regard to the possibility
of having and rearing children. The family you make for yourself will
be—for better, for worse—the group which will be far and away the
most important in your life for determining your happiness or unhappi-
ness and that of the people with whom you will be intimately connected.
It is better for everyone concerned that it should be happiness.

The chief duties in the family are those of parents for their children;
to see that they enjoy a secure and happy childhood and are given a
good preparation for their own lives. Strictly speaking, children owe
no duties to their parents, excepting of the kind engendered by recip-
rocal love, and parents should avoid dependence upon their children
and should not impose obligations upon them. However, natural love
and loyalty lead, in most families, to mutual understanding, mutual
consideration, and, when necessary, mutual aid.

Go halfway to meet your parents in this attempt at understanding.
Remember, when they are raging about your independence, that a)
they are worried and anxious about you, and b) they may be, without
being altogether aware of it, emotionally dependent upon you,
emotionally attached to you—and you could be tactful in accomplish-
ing the new degree of disengagement. Tact is a good thing from both
directions. Bear in mind that: if there is one thing that is more exaspera-
ting than being a suffering teenager, it is being the parent of a suffering
teenager.

8. KEEP THE LAW:

Regard responsibly undertaken crime, delinquency, and hooli-
ganism as—what it is—a mean, petty activity of the unintelligent and
stupid. If there are those (which I still find difficult to believe) who
really do believe that the whole of society is against them and who
resent and reject it, and think it smart to register disapproval by antisocial behaviour then get rid of the idea. The law exists for positive

reasons: to ensure the social order which is necessary for a maximum degree of liberty and personal fulfilment. If you find it sadly lacking in many ways (which it is), then try to improve it, and everyone will be on your side. But do not think it an assertion of independence or freedom or manhood, to steal, or to hit someone with a bicycle chain.

Only those who are ignorant and shortsighted can possibly persuade themselves that crime is smart.

9. COMMIT YOURSELF TO ACTIVE CITIZENSHIP:

It is important to realize that individualism and the achievement of a rich inward personal life, cannot be attained by escaping into isolated living.

By citizenship I mean the art of living, learning, judging and acting co-operatively in order to achieve and sustain a social order which makes possible the maximum opportunity for the fulfilment and enrichment of individual lives. Properly understood, the concern for the social order and the concern for individual values are two sides of the same coin of good human character.

10. HAVE CONFIDENCE IN THE MODERN WORLD AND IN YOUR POWERS TO IMPROVE IT.

It is not true that the conflicts and perplexities of the modern world are an outcome of greater human evil. They are chiefly the outcome of the most rapid and complicated social change that mankind has ever experienced. Industrialization is inevitably bringing together societies of all levels of development. Science is producing a body of new knowledge and a critical attitude of mind which must inevitably disturb traditional beliefs and values. No wonder that our problems are great and that the political situation is dangerous. But the very factors which are producing the problems also give mankind the wherewithal to solve them.

But it is an age of realistic humanitarianism in which the effective improvement of the human condition is an intensely felt aim. Many of our perplexities are due, not to moral evil, but to insufficiently considered moral intensity. The ideals above have not been thoroughly tried and found wanting; we have moved some considerable way towards them, but not far enough. Justice, Liberty, Equality, Fraternity: these, with their implications, are still the best basis on which to organize society. We need a critical appraisal of what has been achieved in these directions and what has not, and then further effort to achieve an order of society approximately more closely to them. This needs hard thinking and hard work. It may not sound very inspiring. The aim of improving the human condition and of attaining excellence in human endeavours and in human character has been the most inspiring ideal of mankind since critical thought began. In the 20th century the very problems that crowd upon us, forcing us to give urgent realistic thought to their solution, mean that we now have it within our grasp actually to achieve in our social institutions, in our concrete day-to-day life, those ideals which, in the entire past of mankind, men and women have been able only to long for—as distant, unattainable goals.

Feel and believe—what is certainly true—that the present age is, in spite of its many gloomy aspects, full of the promise of great achievements in which each person can play a significant and important part.

See that the world does not end, either with a bang or a whimper, but lives a happier life.